M000035163

PURPLE GOLDFISH

10 WAYS TO ATTRACT RAVING CUSTOMERS

STAN PHELPS

&

EVAN CARROLL

© 2019 by Stan Phelps and Evan Carroll

All rights reserved. No part of this work covered by the copyright herein may be reproduced, transmitted, stored, or used in any form including but not limited to photocopying, recording, scanning, digitizing, taping, web distribution, information networks, information storage, or retrieval systems, except as permitted by Section 107 or 108 of the 1976 Copyright Act, without the prior written permission of the publisher.

Published by 9 INCH Marketing

Editing by Lee Heinrich of Write Way Publishing
Cover Design by Joshua Vaughan of Blue Barn Design Co.
Interior Layout by Evan Carroll

ISBN: 978-1-7326652-5-5

First Printing: 2019

Printed in the United States of America

Purple Goldfish 2.0 is available for bulk orders. For further details and special pricing, please email: stan@purplegoldfish.com or call +1.919.360.4702.

This book is dedicated to my beautiful wife Jenn and our two boys, Thomas and James. Their support and love made the original Purple Goldfish Project and the last decade of chasing Goldfish possible.

— Stan Phelps

This book is dedicated to my niece and nephews, Addyson, Zachary, and Sawyer.

— Evan Carroll

CONTENTS

FOREWORD

BY RUSS KLEIN

I used to believe that a brand = the promise + the experience. In fact, marketers had spent more than 75 years in the promise-making business, albeit with little commitment to the brand-building experience. Then brands like Starbucks came along and shook up the status quo, building their brand primarily through experience—with little promise-making. Of course, many have since followed suit. Today's consumers pay little attention to the promises brands make, believing instead authentic stories about what others have experienced. While modern marketers can't control the story, we absolutely can control the experience. And customers will reward great experiences by sharing positive stories about brands that, in turn, become the brand itself.

Today's brand formula reflects my new belief: brand = experience to the power of story.

$$\text{Brand} = \text{Experience}^{\text{STORY}}$$

When it comes to brands, the story factor isn't about storytelling alone, it's a realization that a brand's story is now co-created—and, as a result, not entirely in a marketer's control. As Stan and Evan share in Purple Goldfish 2.0, "Your brand is no longer just what you tell people it is. It's what your customer experiences, how they feel, and, most importantly—what they tell others about that experience."

As marketers, we must take notice—or else. I'm here to disabuse all marketers of the idea that clients need more artful or emotional storytelling. Today's marketers are addicted to storytelling. The advent of content marketing has been the equivalent of a speedball coursing through the craving veins of marketers who think every problem can be solved by telling a better story. Soon they're going to miss a window of opportunity—one that will quickly end up in someone else's portfolio. If marketers don't come to terms with the structural factors that have set the stage for experience-driven brand building in a hurry, CEOs will tap other resources to get it done.

It's all about experience. Experience design is the next frontier for brand building. It's on the fast track to become the most revered marketing capability for any—and every—brand. This idea is at the heart of *Purple Goldfish 2.0*. Smart brands will find ways to add signature value to their experiences, enhancing differentiation and giving customers a reason to share their own stories about brands.

Experience design spares people the effort traditionally needed to enjoy a product or service, with a bias toward removing friction while elegantly layering in relevant enhancements. It combines the disciplines of design thinking and decision science, intentionally applied to the lives of people.

Experience design is probably not what you think it is. Experience design is not just customer service, service recovery, or a digital phenomenon (despite the term "user experience" being coined by Apple in 1993). It's so much more.

World-class experience design—as outlined in this book...

• is intentional.

- is human-centered.

- feels like a story worth telling/is indivisible from storytelling.

- is impressionable, remarkable, unforgettable, and shareable.

- is relevant and differentiating.

- is coherent, repeatable, systematic, and cultural.

- is omni-channel and seamless with no dead ends.

- has fastidious attention to detail.

Want more? You've come to the right place. *Purple Goldfish 2.0* walks you through 10 ways to attract raving customers. This advice is more valuable than ever before. Why? Today, people describe their experience with a brand more than the product or price. More than 80 percent of consumers would pay 25 percent more to ensure a superior experience! More than 80 percent of consumers will stop doing business due to bad experiences with a business. And nearly 80 percent of consumers share bad experiences—warning others, discouraging others, and venting about their negative experiences with brands. The performance data of companies that take an intentional approach to experience design is clear: Happier customers. Higher retention. More profitability.

Everyone is talking about the role of design thinking as part of the marketer's expanding skill set. My advice on experience design is this: Remember brands don't design experiences—they design for experiences. The "dirt path" a customer is taking is likely there because it's now permanently etched into their habits. Stop trying to force them onto a sidewalk when they would prefer you plant flowers along their dirt path.

Purple Goldfish 2.0 provides both inspiration and guidance for marketers seeking to up their game—and their results—by getting serious about experience design. Once they've shown you how great brands are using intentional experience design to build their own brands, Stan and Evan will light your fire to do the same for your brand. But wait, there's more! Stan and Evan wouldn't dream of leaving you without a roadmap. Their I.D.E.A. process will help you design your own Purple Goldfish and add signature extras to your own customer experiences.

This book is your game-changing guide to leveraging the new equation for brand building: experience to the power of story. Game on!

Russ Klein
CEO, American Marketing Association
Award-winning CMO, Dr. Pepper/7UP, Burger King, Arby's

FOREWORD TO THE FIRST EDITION

BY DREW MCLELLAN

Have you ever met someone and within minutes of your first contact, you knew that you were kindred spirits? That's how I felt when Stan first reached out to introduce himself.

We first met a decade ago when he was a brand new blogger. But I knew in an instant that he wasn't brand new to marketing. He got it. Like most people will never get it—Stan got the secret to marketing success.

He understood that marketing is about being so remarkable that people can't help but talk about you. That if you absolutely delight someone—they will not only come back but they'll bring friends. They become your sales force.

Stan delivers this marketing truth over and over again in this book all wrapped in the idea of lagniappe. What's so awesome about the whole notion of Purple Goldfish is that it not only teaches us what to do but more importantly it reminds us that it must be done from the heart.

True lagniappe can't be faked or forced. We banter the word authentic around too much these days. But for lagniappe to work, it must be just that—real and offered without expectation of anything in return.

In other words—you do it because you want to, not because it's in a marketing plan document or because your ROI calculator told you it would generate a 42.36% return. (And no … there's no such thing as an ROI calculator!)

As you read the stories that Stan has collected for this book, I think you're going to be amazed at the creativity and generosity that many businesses have and, in the end, I suspect you'll be inspired to let your inner spirit of lagniappe loose.

You'll probably fill up a notepad with ideas of how you could do a little something extra to enchant your customers. When you've turned that corner and are thinking about them rather than what's in it for you, you're truly ready to practice lagniappe.

I honestly believe that the guys in the white hats do win in the end. And companies that embrace the belief that if you give first and you give generously, you will earn customers for life are marketing's good guys. This book shows us time and time again how to make that happen.

In the end, this book is Stan's own lagniappe for all of us. A genuine gesture of sharing what he truly believes with the hope that it is of great value to us. I'm so happy for you that you've found Stan, his book and are about to receive a gift that could, if you let it, change how you do business forever.

Enjoy!

Drew

INTRODUCTION

BY STAN PHELPS

"Notice the small things. The rewards are inversely proportional."

- Liz Vassey

Purple Goldfish 2.0 is not your ordinary business book. It fundamentally aims to change the paradigm of what we do in business and how we do it.

We've lost focus in marketing. We've been so laser-focused on automating our marketing to prospects that we've forgotten to deliver an exceptional experience once they've become customers. Advertising is no longer the answer. Traditional media is expensive, fragmented, and for the most part ineffective. Customer support is non-existent. We're too busy outsourcing it. We've developed complex loyalty programs that confuse customers and only promise future benefits. What we really need is a concept that differentiates our brand, promotes retention, and generates word of mouth at the time of purchase. We call that concept a Purple Goldfish.

TURNING BACK THE CLOCK

I was first introduced to the concept of lagniappe (pronounced lan-yap) back in 2003 when I was part of a group called *"on the edge."* The group consisted of five guys who would meet every couple of weeks to discuss life and our pursuit of pushing boundaries to stay ... *"on the edge."* I can distinctly remember the night fellow member

Gene Seidman introduced the creole word. Gene explained that lagniappe was the practice of the merchant giving "a little something extra" at the time of purchase. He shared that in Louisiana the word is part of the everyday vernacular. Any time someone goes above and beyond, that's lagniappe.

It was one of those rare things that just clicked when I heard it. Over the next five years, I would share the concept with friends and subconsciously I began looking for examples in my day-to-day life. What I found was that very few businesses understood the concept of going above and beyond by giving little unexpected extras.

ENTER NORWALK, STEW'S, AND RITCHIE

The same year I heard about lagniappe I moved from Amsterdam to Connecticut. My wife Jennifer and I moved to Norwalk, a small city about one hour from Manhattan. Our first house was just up the hill from the most profitable grocery store in the US per square foot according to the *Guinness Book of World Records*.[1] Stew Leonard's was founded by its namesake in 1969. If there is one place I've been that gets the concept of Purple Goldfish, it's Stew Leonard's. We'll visit Stew's multiple times in this book.

The house we bought in Norwalk was a beautiful old stone colonial that we refer to as "Het Stenin Haus" (Dutch for "The Stone House"). Did I mention the house was charming and old? In the first five years, we renovated the kitchen, upgraded the bathrooms, replaced the windows, overhauled the sleeping porch, landscaped the backyard, and refinished the third floor. The first project was the kitchen. A total gut and rebuild. Our contractor, Brian, hired a helper to patch and paint as the job was concluding. The helper

---

1. https://www.inc.com/leigh-buchanan/stew-leonards-400-million-dollar-supermarket-business-main-street.html

referred to himself as Ritchie. Ritchie moved over with his family from Bosnia. Ritchie was a quiet, nice guy with an engaging toothy smile. Even though he was doing a small finishing job, you could tell he took great pride in his work. Ritchie's true specialty was plastering and taping.

One day I came home and found Ritchie patching a crack in the ceiling of our back hallway next to the kitchen. I was a little taken aback and at first a little defensive. This wasn't part of the job and I saw a bill coming. Ritchie just smiled and said not to worry as he was doing it for free. He saw that it needed to be fixed and had some extra material. That little extra made quite an impression. Guess who was top of mind when we had our next painting project? We developed a long-term relationship with Ritchie. Over the next three years, we would engage him on almost every project in our house. Each time he exceeded our expectations and did a little something extra. Ritchie turned a couple-hundred-dollar job into cumulative jobs that earned him tens of thousands of dollars.

THE LONGEST AND HARDEST NINE INCHES IN MARKETING

In 2008, I was working as part of the leadership team for an experiential marketing agency. We created larger than life product launches, PR stunts, sponsorship activations, and mobile tours. The goal was to create signature experiences that drove impressions through earned media. Many of our activations were successful, some even went viral and won awards. But they were neither scalable nor sustainable. I became disenchanted with this type of marketing. I thought there had to be a better way. So, I launched a blog called 9 Inch Marketing. The goal was to write and discover

50 marketing axioms. I was searching for a game changing concept in business.

Disclaimer: Nothing personal with the 9 Inch reference I assure you. Nine inches is the average distance between the brain and the heart. Those nine inches are personal to 85 percent of the people reading this book. Spread your hand out and stretch your fingers as wide as they'll go. Now place your fingers along the spine of this book. The distance between your thumb and pinky is exactly nine inches or 23 centimeters. I refer to those nine inches as the "longest and hardest" for any marketer, given the ultimate goal of winning the heart of your customer.

My first dedicated post was about the concept of lagniappe. With each post I included a small section called "Today's Lagniappe" with a fun extra bit of trivia, a joke, or a story. My first guest post on another blog, Drew McLellan's *Drew's Marketing Minute,* was about the concept of lagniappe. My first SlideShare presentation was also about the concept of lagniappe.

In September 2009, I experienced what I call my moment of truth in New York City. We'll address that in the first chapter. It spurred a post highlighting a concept I called a Purple Goldfish. That post would be the spark plug that ignited my passion and became the impetus for starting the Purple Goldfish Project. The project hosted on List.ly[2] was an ambitious attempt to crowd source 1,001 examples of Purple Goldfish. Early in 2010, I started a video podcast with Jack Campisi. The ball was rolling.

The original *Purple Goldfish* book was launched in January of 2012. It had taken 27 months to reach the goal of collecting 1,001 examples. That year our family moved from Connecticut to Cary,

---

2. https://list.ly/list/1Ni-purple-goldfish-project

North Carolina. BANG! As Mike Michalowicz has coined, I started to pursue my Big Audacious Noble Goal.[3] Being the single income in our family, I cashed in over $100,000 in my 401(K) and left my agency role as EVP and Chief Solutions Officer. I embarked on the journey of being an author and speaker. My "BANG" was to change the paradigm of business. To challenge leaders to think about the customer they had as opposed to focusing on chasing the prospect they wanted. I wanted to inspire them to go beyond the transaction and honor the relationship and to focus on an experience that would win customers and influence word of mouth. In the words of Peter Shankman, "Taking care of the customers you have ... so they'll bring you the customers you want."

WHAT'S OLD IS NEW AGAIN

This idea of doing little extras is not new. We'll trace its US origins to the 1800s. Sometimes it can help spawn a business. For example, do you know the story of a boy from upstate New York named David McConnell? In 1874, at the age of 16, David started to sell books door-to-door. When his fare was not well received, McConnell resorted to a little extra. David would promise a free gift in exchange for being allowed to make a sales pitch. The "little something extra" was a complimentary vial of perfume. It was a signature extra as David concocted his original scent with the aid of a local pharmacist. McConnell quickly learned his customers adored his perfume yet remained indifferent to his books.[4] Soon he would concentrate solely on cosmetics, starting a company called the California Perfume Company. In 1886, it would become Avon Cosmetics. Ding-dong. Who knew the first Avon Lady was actually a boy? Despite competition from hundreds of American and foreign brand name

---

3. https://mikemichalowicz.com/how-noble-are-your-goals/

4. https://about.avon.com/avon-about-us/company/founder.html

cosmetics today, Avon remains a leader with Avon Ladies ringing doorbells coast to coast.

Or do you know the story about a social worker with a passion for good food and a commitment to healthy living? In 1996, without the capital to open a restaurant, Stacy Madison and her husband began serving healthy pita bread roll-up sandwiches. Their lunch cart in Boston's Financial District became popular and soon lines started to form around the block. To make waiting more palatable (literally), Stacy concocted a little extra for customers waiting in line. Each night she baked leftover pita bread sprinkled with seasoning to create different flavored chips. The chips were a huge hit and soon Stacy's Pita Chip Company was born.[5] Stacy's experienced rapid growth, doubling sales every year, which led to a multimillion dollar acquisition by Frito Lay.

A SERIES IS BORN

The original *Purple Goldfish* book in 2012 started my journey. In studying over 1,000 examples and over 500 brands, it quickly became apparent to me that customers were only part of the equation in customer experience. I found that the companies who really got "it" for the customers put an even greater emphasis on engaging their own employees. In the words of Ted Coiné in the foreword of *Green Goldfish 2.0* (co-authored with Lauren McGhee), "You can't have happy enthused customers without happy engaged employees." Gold in 2014 was the third color in the original trilogy that was inspired by the three colors of Mardi Gras (purple, green, and gold). *Golden Goldfish* explored the idea that all customers and employees are not created equal. The top 20 percent of customers drive 80 percent of profits. *Blue Goldfish* (co-authored with Evan Carroll)

---

5. https://www.americanexpress.com/en-us/business/trends-and-insights/articles/the-story-behind-stacys-pita-chips/

was next in 2016. It explored the impact of technology, data, and analytics on customer experience. The fifth color, *Red Goldfish* (co-authored with Graeme Newell in 2017), explored how being "for purpose" creates loyalty for customers and employees. *Pink Goldfish* (co-authored with David Rendall) returned to the marketing roots of Purple in 2018. It examined differentiation and how to create competitive separation in business by exploiting weirdness and weakness to captivate customers and stand out in a sea of sameness. The seventh color, also in 2018, was Yellow. *Yellow Goldfish* (co-authored with Rosaria Cirillo Louwman) looked at how companies can do a little extra to contribute to the happiness of their customers, employees, and society. The eighth color is Gray. *Gray Goldfish* in 2019 (co-authored with Brian Doyle) was the first Goldfish book on effective leadership and focused on how to navigate five generations in the workplace.

RETHINKING PURPLE

I've teamed up with Evan Carroll for this relaunch called *Purple Goldfish 2.0*. Evan was my first co-author in the *Goldfish book series*. Since we wrote *Blue Goldfish* together in 2016, he has been an integral part of developing the subsequent colors. We met back in 2013 through the American Marketing Association. I volunteered to be the Director of Special Events for the Triangle Chapter. I worked with Evan as he founded the High Five Conference in Raleigh. The inaugural event was in February 2014. It was a bonding experience. The next year I would become President-Elect as Evan served as President for the Triangle Chapter. *Blue Goldfish* launched in 2016 and that summer we embarked on a cross-country speaking tour. [Sidebar: If you ever think about doing a cross-country road trip, here's some advice ... start with a small country.] That same year Evan also helped co-create the full-day Purple Goldfish workshop.

In 2017, we developed the annual *"Think Outside the Bowl"* conference. In 2018, we would once again jump in the car for a three-week summer speaking tour. I can't think of a better person to join me on this updated version. With a strong background in brand marketing, product management, user experience design, and customer experience, he has helped improve the 2.0 version of Purple Goldfish immensely.

Let's get started...

PREFACE

"In marketing I've seen only one strategy that can't miss—and that is to market to your best customers first, your best prospects second and the rest of the world last."

- John Romero

MARKETING IS CHANGING FOR THE BETTER ...

One could make the assertion that marketing has changed more in the last decade than it has in the previous 100 years. Power has shifted. The consumer has a bigger voice and traditional "tell and sell" marketing is waning. It's important to recognize the direction of key changes taking place.

LET'S COUNTDOWN THE TOP 10 WAYS MARKETING IS CHANGING:

10. Retention is becoming the new acquisition in marketing.

It now costs up to 10 times the amount of money to acquire a new customer than it does to keep a current one.[6]

9. We heard it through the grapevine.

WOMMA and the American Marketing Association found that 64 percent of marketing executives indicated that they believe word

---

6. https://hbr.org/2014/10/the-value-of-keeping-the-right-customers

of mouth is the most effective form of marketing. However, only 6 percent say they have mastered it.[7]

8. Zip it or Zap it?

Today, 86 percent of consumers skip TV ads.[8]

7. There is always an alternative.

Over 70 percent of consumers will abandon a brand because of a bad customer experience.[9]

6. Consumers don't know what they like.

They like what they know or what their friends know. According to McKinsey, 67 percent of all consumer decisions are primarily influenced by word of mouth.[10]

5. Pardon the Interruption.

In the 1970s, the average consumer was exposed to 500 to 2,000 messages a day. Today, it ranges between 3,000 and 5,000 per day.[11]

4. Love is a battlefield for customers and marketing.

Gartner reports that 89 percent of business leaders say customer experience is the new battlefield and the number one thing they'll compete on. Pat Benatar could not be reached for comment.[12]

7. https://www.forbes.com/sites/kimberlywhitler/2014/07/17/why-word-of-mouth-marketing-is-the-most-important-social-media/

8. https://www.cnbc.com/2017/01/11/generation-z-avoids-advertising-uses-ad-blockers-and-skips-content.html

9. https://www.forbes.com/sites/sap/2017/09/28/47-percent-of-consumers-will-abandon-your-brand-for-one-reason/

10. https://www.prdaily.com/report-83-percent-say-word-of-mouth-influences-their-purchases/

11. https://www.gradschools.com/programs/marketing-advertising/how-many-ads-do-you-see-each-day

12. https://www.gartner.com/smarterwithgartner/customer-experience-battlefield/

3. Forget the water cooler.

Social has become a game changer. Today's satisfied customer tells three friends; a pissed off customer tells 3,000.[13]

2. Likelihood to buy.

Customers referred by friends are prone to trust the company more and are four times more likely to buy.[14]

And the #1 reason marketing is changing...

1. Search is a game changer.

Forget about your cross-town rival, your competition is now just one click away.

13. Blackshaw, Pete. Satisfied Customers Tell Three Friends, Angry Customers Tell 3,000: Running a Business in Today's Consumer-Driven World. Crown Business, 2008.

14. https://www.talkable.com/blog/referral-marketing-most-efficient-strategy/

THE PURPLE GOLDFISH
(THE WHY)

CHAPTER 1

THE BIGGEST MYTH
IN MARKETING

"The search for meaningful distinction is central to the marketing effort. If marketing is about anything, it is about achieving customer-getting distinction by differentiating what you do and how you operate. All else is derivative of that and only that."

-Theodore Levitt

TALL TALES FROM NYC

A decade ago, Stan was in New York City with a colleague. He and his colleague Brad were at a trendy hotel rooftop bar. One of those places where a bottle of beer is $15. (Sidebar: Is it possible to enjoy a beer that costs $15?) They were waiting to meet a few people before heading over to a networking event. There was an older gentleman sitting right across from them. It was obvious that he was waiting for someone. Stan decided to strike up a conversation about waiting. He leaned over and asked the older man, "Do you know that we spend 10 percent of our life waiting?" He then told the man that because he had once read it on the Internet, it had to be true.

They both laughed and began talking about etiquette. Stan stressed the importance of being on time. He shared legendary coach Vince Lombardi's stance on timeliness. Lombardi Time is the idea of showing up 15 minutes ahead of the scheduled meeting time. Not on time, but 15 minutes early. If folks meeting with him weren't 15 minutes early, Coach Lombardi considered them "late." Right then this guy shook his head and said to Stan and Brad, "There is no such thing as being on time."

In disbelief, Stan said, "Wait a second, I've been on time before." The older man raised his hand and began waving his finger back and forth. Just like the former NBA star Dikembe Mutumbo and his famous finger wave. He exclaimed, "No, no, no. Being on time is a fallacy. No one is ever on time. On time is a myth. You either are early or you are late."

This was a complete paradigm shift for Stan. That night he began thinking about how this fallacy applies to marketing and meeting customer expectations. He always thought that the idea of meeting expectations was a surefire recipe for losing business. It almost guarantees you will fall short. It's similar to playing prevent defense in football. Prevent defense only prevents you from doing one thing—winning.

This new paradigm only made it clearer. Meeting expectations is the biggest myth in business. Santa Claus, the Tooth Fairy, and Meeting Expectations. Kids, cover your eyes and ears—they are all myths.

In business you either fall below expectations or you exceed them. There is no middle ground. It bears repeating: There is no such thing as meeting expectations.

A world where 60 to 80 percent of customers describe their customer satisfaction as satisfied or very satisfied—right before they defect to other brands—shows that simply "meeting expectations" is no longer an option.

Stan woke up the next morning and started thinking about companies that purposely set out to exceed the expectations of their customers. The Purple Goldfish Project and the quest to find 1,001 examples was born.

THERE ARE TWO PATHS

There are two paths that diverge in the business woods. Many companies take the wide first path and are happy with meeting expectations. Others consciously take the narrower and tougher road, deciding to go above and beyond to do more than reasonably expected.

Seth Godin wrote about this in the post "Once in a Lifetime." He touches on these two paths:

> This is perhaps the greatest marketing strategy struggle of our time: Should your product or service be

very good, meet spec and be beyond reproach or ... should it be a remarkable, memorable, over the top, a tell-your-friends event? The answer isn't obvious, and many organizations are really conflicted about this. Delta Airlines isn't trying to make your day. They're trying to get you from Atlanta to Salt Lake City, close to on time, less expensive than the other guy, and hopefully without hassle. That's a win for them. Most of the consumer businesses (restaurants, services, etc.) and virtually all of the business to business ventures I encounter, shoot for the first (meeting spec). They define spec and they work to achieve it. A few, from event organizers to investment advisors, work every single day to create over-the-top remarkable experiences. It's a lot of work, and it requires passion.

Godin outlines the choice of meeting spec or going above and beyond. Your business strategy defines which path you will take. The worst place to be is in the mushy middle. Your decision boils down to the simple issue of meeting expectations. If all you want to do is meet expectations, then you are setting yourself up to become a commodity. If you are not willing to differentiate yourself by creating valuable experiences or little touches that go "above and beyond" for your customer, you will languish in the sea of sameness. We challenge you to choose your path wisely.

TO UNDER-DELIVER OR OVER-DELIVER, THAT IS THE QUESTION

In today's climate you need to stand out by answering two important questions:

1. *What is valued by your customers?*

2. *Can you deliver on those things that are valued and create some signature elements of added value to create differentiation?*

Creating small unexpected extras can go a long way to increasing retention, promoting loyalty, and generating positive word of mouth. Investing in current customers is the lowest hanging fruit in marketing. Conversely, focusing solely on prospects in the purchase funnel and neglecting actual customer experience is a recipe for disaster.

SHAREHOLDERS VS. CUSTOMERS—WHO COMES FIRST?

Why are corporations in business? There are two sides of the argument:

1. Milton Friedman's theory is that the sole purpose of a corporation is to drive shareholder value. "There is one and only one social responsibility of business," Friedman wrote back in 1970, and that is to "engage in activities designed to increase profits."[15]

2. Theodore "Ted" Levitt's theory is that companies are solely in the business of getting and keeping customers. "Not so long ago companies assumed the purpose of a business is to make money. But that has proved as vacuous as saying the purpose of life is to eat … The purpose of a business is to create and keep a customer."[16]

We believe Levitt is correct. Companies should focus on customers and how to create competitive separation. In Levitt's words, "The search for meaningful distinction is central to the marketing effort. If marketing is about anything, it is about achieving customer-getting

---

15. https://www.nytimes.com/1970/09/13/archives/a-friedman-doctrine-the-social-responsibility-of-business-is-to.html

16. Levitt, Theodore. Marketing Imagination: New, Expanded Edition, New York: Simon and Schuster, 1986.

distinction by differentiating what you do and how you operate. All else is derivative of that and only that."

FOCUS ON THE CUSTOMER OR THE BOTTOM LINE?

For the last century and a half, the vast majority of corporations focused solely on the bottom line. The approach has been win at all cost with little or no regard for external effects, collateral damage, or customer experience. The problem is that only pursuing the bottom line can neglect the customer. This was outlined in an article from *Harvard Business Review* by James Allen, Frederick Reichheld, and Barney Hamilton:

> Call it the dominance trap: The larger a company's market share, the greater the risk it will take its customers for granted. As the money flows in, management begins confusing customer profitability with customer loyalty, never realizing that the most lucrative buyers may also be the angriest and most alienated. Worse, traditional market research may lead the firm to view customers as statistics. Managers can become so focused on the data that they stop hearing the real voices of their customers.[17]

The entire premise of *Purple Goldfish 2.0* is that the customer must come first. Customer experience should be the biggest priority. Stop focusing on "the two in the bush" (prospects) and take care of "the one in your hand" (your customer). Take care of the customers you have. When you provide them with a memorable experience, they'll bring you the customers you want.

---

17. https://hbswk.hbs.edu/archive/the-three-ds-of-customer-experience

CHAPTER 2

WARMTH, COMPETENCE, AND WORD OF MOUTH

"If you love your customers,
your customers will love you back."

- Stew Leonard

Stew Leonard grew up the son of a dairy farmer in Connecticut. In the 1960s, he began working for the family business. Clover Farms Dairy delivered milk to customers' homes. Two events would alter the trajectory of his life and the business. The first was the decline in demand for milk delivery. The second was that the family dairy farm was lost to the State. Connecticut invoked eminent domain, taking the dairy farm property to build a new highway called Route 7 in Norwalk. Stew was forced to pivot. The result was the opening of his first dairy store in Norwalk in 1969.

During the first year the store was open, Stew was asked by the local elementary principal to speak at an upcoming Career Day. The principal asked Stew to talk about his store and the dairy business. Even though Stew didn't see the appeal for kids, he reluctantly agreed. That Friday morning, he drove to the school. As Stew pulled into the parking lot, he immediately knew he was in trouble. There was a fire truck parked in front of the school with kids all around it. It didn't get any better when he walked through the doors of the school. He immediately saw a room with an Air Force officer. A movie about the history of jet airplanes was playing. It was filled with kids. Across the hall was a police officer, and he was showing a packed classroom about various police equipment and weapons. Stew proceeded to walk down the hall and eventually found his classroom. There was a sign on the door that read: **The Milk Business**.

Stew walked in the room to find only three kids sitting inside. Two of them were the sons of his produce manager. For the next 30 minutes he talked about the dairy business and running a store. At the end of the talk he thanked the kids. Stew then reached into his pocket and handed them each a coupon for a free ice cream. The kids left and Stew waited to present the second of his two Career Day sessions. He waited and waited. No kids. After 10 minutes, no one had showed up. After 15 minutes passed, not one kid had arrived. After 20 minutes, the principal came rushing in and franti-cally exclaimed, "Stew, I don't know what you told those kids, but we have to move your next presentation to the school auditorium."

This simple story underscores the power of giving little unexpected extras and how effective word of mouth marketing can be. This event would shape Stew's thinking on the importance of word of mouth marketing and the importance of doing little unexpected extras. To this day, when you visit Stew Leonard's and buy $100 or more in groceries, you will receive a free ice cream. If you don't like ice cream, you can show your receipt for a free cup of coffee. Buy $200 and you get two ice creams or coffees. It's just one of many examples of a Purple Goldfish from Stew Leonard's.

WHY DID THOSE KIDS REACT SO STRONGLY?

The word traveled quickly about Stew's coupon for a free ice cream. Why did this small gift move the needle? A big part of the reason has to do with how our brain evolved as humans. As we evolved, we were forced to develop skills integral to our survival. One of those skills was the ability to make snap judgments about our sur-roundings with a high degree of speed and accuracy. As we walked out of the cave, our senses went immediately into survival mode. We judged everyone and everything we encountered on two basic criteria:

1. Warmth: What is their intent? Are they a threat?

2. Competence: What is their ability to carry out that intent?

This basic truth is at the heart of Chris Malone and Susan T. Fiske's book, *The Human Brand*.[18] Their research, built upon work done

18. Malone, Chris, and Susan T. Fiske. The Human Brand: How We Relate to People, Products, and Companies. San Francisco: Jossey-Bass, 2014.

by Dr. Bogdan Wojciszke,[19] has shown that over 80 percent of our judgments are based on these two factors of warmth and competence. These perceptions don't just apply to people. We also apply the same standards to products and companies. We automatically perceive and judge their behaviors on a subconscious level. Brands are people too.

FROM THE LOCAL VILLAGE TO MASS MARKET TO GLOBAL VILLAGE

The mass market we know today is a relatively new phenomenon. It only began 150 years ago. Before the industrial revolution, nearly everything we consumed was made by people we knew. The reputation of a merchant was as precious as gold. If a small business wronged someone, everyone in the local village would know about it by Sunday services. Merchants faced public censure, potential ruin, and even losing a limb (as we'll find out in chapter four). As a result, businesses worked hard to establish trust and earn repeat business. Business was about relationships and not just transactions.

But then the mass market emerged, and the modern corporation was born. Almost everything we consume today is made by a faceless, far-off company. The voice of the customer waned. We were powerless to expose or punish brands that acted badly. Outside of lodging a complaint with the Better Business Bureau or consumer advocates like Ralph Nader, we were handcuffed.

Enter Digital, Social, and Mobile over the last 15 years. The Internet and global connectivity have changed the game. In the words of author Chris Malone, "For the first time in history, the entire world is wired in a way that is consistent with the way evolution has wired us to think and behave." Social has flattened the earth.

19. https://wojciszke.socialpsychology.org/

Consumers have the opportunity to share their experiences with millions of others, causing a huge ripple effect in the global village.

Customers want to be heard. Social accountability is back—and it's here to stay. Customers expect to have relationships with their brands. Companies must forge genuine relationships with customers. We now expect relational accountability from the companies and brands we support. Malone and Fiske call this a "Relationship Renaissance."

BRINGING WARMTH AND COMPETENCE TO LIFE

Consumers will view the actions (or inaction) of brands based on warmth and competence. And warmth is absolutely key. Need an example to drive this home? Are you familiar with the story of Panera and Brandon Cook?

In the summer of 2012, Brandon Cook was visiting with his grandmother. She was in the hospital in New Hampshire and the prognosis was dire. Brandon's grandmother had pancreatic cancer and was down to her last few days. One of the horrible side effects of pancreatic cancer is that you get to the point where you can no longer eat. Brandon was watching his grandmother suffer, and he was pleading with her to have something to eat. After the consistent pleading, Brandon's grandmother said, "I'd like to have some soup." She then qualified her request. "But not the soup they serve at the hospital," she said. She wanted a bread bowl of clam chowder.

Where do you get a bread bowl of clam chowder? You get it at Panera. But here was the problem. Due to demand, Panera only serves clam chowder on Fridays during the summer. This was a Monday. Brandon wasn't going to let that get in the way. Being the millennial that he was, he simply picked up his phone and called the closest Panera in Nashua. Within a minute, he was speaking to Sue, the manager at Panera. Brandon explained the situation and his grandmother's wishes. Upon hearing the story, Sue stopped Brandon and told him to come over. They would be happy to help him and his grandmother. Brandon drove the 10 minutes to Panera and met Sue and her team. They gave Brandon a couple bread bowls of clam chowder. As a little extra, they also threw in a small box of cookies for them to share.

Brandon returned to the hospital and had a wonderful lunch with his grandmother. For a short time, it sustained her and made her happy. Driving home that afternoon, Brandon reflected on this small act of kindness by Panera. He decided he was going to do something about it.

How do we know Brandon Cook was a good kid? Well, he must have been as he took the time to visit his grandmother. He was also thoughtful because he fulfilled her clam chowder request. How do we know for sure? We can be 100 percent sure because Brandon was friends with his mom on Facebook. Brandon wrote about his experience on the social networking site. Here is what he shared in the post:

> My grandmother is passing soon with cancer. I visited her the other day and she was telling me about how she really wanted soup, but not hospital soup because she said it tasted "awful" she went on about how she really would like some clam chowder from Panera. Unfortunately, Panera only sells clam chowder on Friday. I called the manager Sue and told [her] the situation. I wasn't looking for anything special just a bowl of clam chowder. Without hesitation she said absolutely she would make her some clam chowder. When I went to pick it up they wound up giving me a box of cookies as well. It's not that big of a deal to most, but to my grandma it meant a lot. I really want

to thank Sue and the rest of the staff from Panera in Nashua NH just for making my grandmother happy. Thank you so much![20]

Brandon's mom, Gail, saw the post and was moved. She copied it and placed it on Panera's Facebook page. That's when something amazing happened. In less than four weeks, a single Facebook post by Brandon Cook had garnered more than 800,000 likes, over 34,000 comments, and scores of national media attention. Why? Because Panera empowered its employees to demonstrate warmth and competence by doing the little extra.

The idea of warmth and competence is not just theory. It draws from original research spanning ten separate studies. Companies need to find ways to leverage individual customer and employee relationships by doing a tangible extra. Actions speak louder than words.

USING PARETO TO FLIP THE RATIO ON TRADITIONAL MARKETING

The setting is Paris 1848. A boy was born to an exiled noble Genoese family. His father, Raffaele, was an Italian civil engineer who had fled Italy like other Italian nationalists. His mother, Marie, was French. Enthusiastic about the German revolution that year, Raffaele and Marie named their son Fritz Wilfried.

Fritz would become Vilfredo upon his family's move back to Italy when he was 10. He would grow up to become an engineer, sociologist, economist, political scientist, and philosopher. During his life he would make several important contributions to economics,

20. https://www.facebook.com/panerabread/posts/my-grandmother-is-passing-soon-with-cancer-i-visited-her-the-other-day-and-she-w/10151080790559629/

particularly in the study of income distribution and in the analysis of individuals' choices.

His legacy as an economist was profound. Vilfredo's books look more like modern economics than most other texts of that day: tables of statistics from across the world and ages, rows of integral signs, and intricate charts/graphs. Partly because of his work, the field of economics evolved from a branch of moral philosophy, as practiced by Adam Smith, into a data intensive field. Vilfredo is perhaps the first data scientist. He is credited with helping to develop the field of microeconomics, becoming the first to discover that income follows a distribution.[21]

In 1907, Vilfredo stumbled across an idea that would change the course of history. This revelation would come from a simple observation from his vegetable garden. While preparing dinner, Vilfredo noticed something peculiar about the peas in his pea pods. This simple observation turned into action. Vilfredo began to pluck all the pods off the plant. He opened each and made an interesting discovery. Vilfredo found that 80 percent of his peas came from a mere 20 percent of his pods. This intrigued the 59-year-old Italian economist.

Soon he was applying this ratio to other socioeconomic scenarios. You may now recognize his last name. His full name was Vilfredo Federico Damaso Pareto. Pareto's most famous finding was that 20 percent of the people in Italy owned 80 percent of the land.

Pareto's discovery and contribution was largely unheralded until two decades after his death. During World War II, social scientist Joseph Juran uncovered his work while streamlining shipment processes for the Lend-Lease Administration in Washington, D.C. Juran was studying defects in shipments. He found that 80 percent

---

21. https://en.wikipedia.org/wiki/Vilfredo_Pareto

of the defects were attributed to just 20 percent of the causes. Juran was the first to coin the phrases, "Pareto's Law of Unequal Distribution" and the "80/20 rule."[22] Pretty soon Juran was applying the rule to a number of scenarios. Here are a few of his findings:

- 80 percent of the World's GDP is controlled by 20 percent of the people.

- 80 percent of the complaints come from 20 percent of the customers.

- 80 percent of a company's sales come from 20 percent of its products.

Juran's most important application came within the field of quality control. He noticed that the majority of defects came from a small percentage of all possible causes. Juran famously referred to Pareto's principle as, "The law of the vital few and the trivial many." It's time to apply this principle to traditional marketing.

ENTER THE GOLDFISH COROLLARY

If we subscribe to the principle that 80 percent of your results will be generated by 20 percent of your efforts, then we respectfully put forth the Goldfish Corollary: 80 percent of your traditional marketing efforts will net you 20 percent of the results.

Today, traditional marketing is woefully ineffective. This attribution phenomenon isn't new. According to the late legendary 19th century retailer Joseph Wanamaker, "Half the money I spend on advertising is wasted … the problem is that I don't know which half."

---

22. https://www.economist.com/news/2009/06/19/joseph-juran

We believe 50 percent is an understatement and therefore propose that the vast majority of marketing dollars spent on the traditional funnel (the 80 percent) will net one dollar worth of return for every four that you spend given the Goldfish 80/20 Corollary.

THE LEAKY BUCKET AND REVOLVING DOOR EFFECT

There is a huge flaw when focusing the majority of your marketing efforts on the traditional purchase funnel. That flaw is The Revolving Door Effect. If the majority of your marketing is mainly focused on prospective customers, you may be able to add between 10 to 25 percent of new customers per year.

"Wait a second ...," most companies would say. "Sign me up right now for an increase of 10 to 25 percent of customers per year." The problem is that most businesses have huge problems with retention. It may not be uncommon to lose 10 to 25 percent of your customer base in a given year. The net effect is that you might negate all of your gains and in essence create a revolving door by not taking care of your new and current customers. A study by Gartner revealed that a five percent decrease in attrition can yield an increase between 25 to 125 percent in bottom line profits.

The overwhelming traditional view of marketing is the process of acquiring prospective customers. It is not uncommon to find companies spending 80 percent of their marketing budgets on getting consumers into the purchase funnel. We've become so preoccupied with generating awareness and interest that we tend to forget about our most important asset, our current customers. We need to flip that ratio on traditional marketing. We need to heed Pareto's Law and determine the 20 percent of traditional marketing we are doing that is generating the strongest ROI. Once you've earmarked that vital 20 percent, it's time to focus a majority of the remaining 80 percent squarely on current customers.

By putting the focus on your current customers, you eliminate waste, drive differentiation, and generate the following three benefits:

- Reduce attrition

- Increase loyalty

- Drive positive word of mouth

STANDING OUT IN A SEA OF SAMENESS

Your brand is no longer what you tell people it is. It's what your customers experience, how they feel about your brand, and, most importantly, what they tell other people about their experience. Great brands know their customers and create an experience that resonates.

Word of mouth is absolutely key to your growth. How are you standing out in a sea of sameness? What are your one or two signature differentiators in customer experience? Instead of being a "me too," what is the one special thing your company does that is superior and distinctive in the eyes of your customers? What is that little something extra that is tangible, valuable, and talkable?

What do you hang your hat on? How do you stand out from your competition?

- What is your warm-chocolate-chip-cookie first impression like DoubleTree Hotels?

- What is your "Bags Fly Free" added value like Southwest Airlines?

- What is your free peanuts and bonus fries like Five Guys?

- What is your free shipping upgrade to overnight like Zappos?

We call these little things Purple Goldfish. Let's explore the metaphor and uncover the background on why a goldfish.

CHAPTER 3

WHY A GOLDFISH?

"The thing that makes something remarkable isn't usually directly related to the original purpose of the product or service.

It's the extra stuff, the stylish bonus, the design or the remarkable service or pricing that makes people talk about it and spread the word."

- Seth Godin

Kimpton Hotels is one part of the inspiration behind the metaphor of goldfish. Kimpton gets the guest experience. The hotel chain has a number of signature additions that go above and beyond expectations. If you stay at a Kimpton, there is always free gourmet coffee in the lobby. There is fresh fruit and in the afternoon the hotel does wine tasting. Not samples—full glasses of wine. Some Kimpton hotels will let you take out a bike for free to tour the city. All Kimptons are pet-friendly. Bring your dog for free and they'll treat your pup like royalty. My favorite little extra was introduced by Kimpton at each Hotel Monaco back in 2001. Perhaps you are staying at a Kimpton and getting a little lonely. Or maybe you and your family are away from home and missing your family pet. The program is called Guppy Love. It offers guests the ability to adopt a temporary travel companion for their stay—a goldfish. This signature program gained the chain national attention. Steve Pinetti, Senior Vice President of Sales & Marketing for Kimpton Hotels and Restaurants, shared:

> The "Guppy Love" program is a fun extension of our pet-friendly nature as well as our emphasis on indulging the senses to heighten the travel experience. Everything about Hotel Monaco appeals directly to the senses, and 'Guppy Love' offers one more unique way to relax, indulge and promote health of mind, body and spirit in our home-away-from-home atmosphere.[23]

The second reason behind a goldfish has to do with Stan's childhood. At age six, his first pet was a goldfish named Oscar. He won it at a fair by throwing a ping pong ball in a carnival game. Oscar was small, maybe one or two inches in length. It turns out that the average goldfish is just over three inches. Yet the largest in the world is just under 20 inches. Not a carp or a koi, an ordinary goldfish. That's more than six times the average size.

---

23. https://purplegoldfish.com/its-always-5-oclock-kimpton/

FACT

The current *Guinness Book of World Records* holder for the largest goldfish hails from the Netherlands at a whopping 19 inches (50 centimeters). To put that in perspective, that's about the size of the average domestic cat.[24]

Six times larger!!! Imagine walking down the street and bumping into someone who's nearly three stories tall. How can there be such a disparity between your garden variety goldfish and their monster cousins?

It turns out that the growth of the goldfish is determined by five factors. And those same five factors also relate to the growth of any business.

Let's unpack the five factors:

#1. The first growth factor for a goldfish is the SIZE OF THE EN-VIRONMENT they are in. The size of the bowl or pond is one determinant of how much they will grow. The size is a direct correlation. The larger the bowl or pond, the larger the goldfish can grow. The smaller the market, the lesser the growth. In business, what's the equivalent of the bowl or the pond? It's simply the MARKET for your product or service.

Takeaway: The bigger the market, the more you can grow.

#2. The second growth factor for a goldfish is the NUMBER OF OTHER GOLDFISH in the environment. This is an inverse correlation. The more goldfish in the bowl or pond, typically the less growth achieved. With fewer goldfish, the more growth

---

24. https://www.guinnessworldrecords.com/world-records/longest-goldfish

opportunity. Who are the other goldfish in business? They are your COMPETITION.

Takeaway: The more competition, the harder it is to grow. The less competition, the easier it is to grow.

#3. The third growth factor is the QUALITY OF THE WATER that the goldfish is in. Nutrients and cloudiness in the water will impact the growth of a goldfish. The better the quality—the more nutrients and less cloudiness in the water—the more growth. Conversely, less nutrients and more cloudiness will hamper growth. What is the equivalent of the quality of water in business? Here we need to think in a macro and environmental sense. The quality of the water is the ECONOMY. It is a direct correlation.

Takeaway: The better the quality of the economy and the greater consumer confidence, the larger the growth. The weaker the economy or capital markets, the more difficult it is to access capital and grow.

FACT

A malnourished goldfish in a crowded, cloudy environment may only grow to two inches (five centimeters).

#4. The fourth factor for a goldfish is how they're treated in the FIRST 120 DAYS of life. The nourishment and treatment they receive as babies are key to future growth. Goldfish are tiny when they are born, usually with about a hundred brothers and sisters. They are about the size of the head of a pin. What do you call a baby goldfish? A baby goldfish is a fry, as in "small fry." The lower the quality of the food and treatment, the more the goldfish will be stunted for future growth. What's the equivalent of the first 120 days in business? A business is typically called a START-UP during its early days in business.

Takeaway: How a start-up does in the first four months of its existence will be a determining factor of how it will do the long term.

#5. The fifth and final growth factor for a goldfish is GENETIC MAKEUP. The strength of its genetics will determine future growth. The stronger its genes and the more it is separated from the rest of the goldfish, the more it typically grows. The poorer the genes and the more it hangs out in the same goldfish group, the less it can grow. What's the equivalent of genetic makeup in business? It is DIFFERENTIATION.

Takeaway: The more differentiated the product or service from the competition, the better the chance for growth. The less differentiated and the more a business is like the competition, the harder it will be to grow.

WHICH OF THE FIVE FACTORS CAN YOU CONTROL?

Let's assume you have an existing product or service and have been in business for more than four months. Which of the remaining four factors do you have control over?

1. Size of the bowl = Market

2. Number of other goldfish = Competition

3. Quality of water = Economy

4. Genetic makeup = Differentiation

Do you have any control over the market, your competition, or the economy? NO, NO, and NO. The only thing you have control over is your business's genetic make-up or how you differentiate your product or service. And how are you going to differentiate? What's the number one thing you are going to compete on? Research by Gartner shared that 89 percent of companies believe that the number one thing they'll compete on is the experience they provide. It's no longer price, location, or even service. It's the entire experience. Gartner asked the same question in 2011. Only 36 percent of companies elected experience as the number one factor. That provides stark evidence on how much more important the experience is today.

CUSTOMER EXPERIENCE IS MORE IMPORTANT THAN EVER

Here are three leading indications of why this is so:

1. The cost of customer acquisition continues to rise, making increasing retention the lowest hanging fruit in marketing.

2. Consumers now have a stronger voice given the emergence of search and social technologies like blogs, Wikis, Facebook, YouTube, Twitter, Instagram, TripAdvisor, and Yelp.

3. Competing solely on price can "commoditize" your product or service.

The goldfish represents the importance of differentiation as a driver of growth. Now let's explore the reasoning behind the color purple.

CHAPTER 4

WHY PURPLE?

"We picked up one excellent word—a word worth traveling to New Orleans to get; a nice limber, expressive, handy word."

- Mark Twain

Purple is an ode to New Orleans, specifically because of its most famous event—Mardi Gras. Purple is one of the three official colors. The selection of the Mardi Gras colors originates from when the Grand Duke Alexis Romanoff of Russia visited New Orleans in 1872. The Grand Duke came to the city in pursuit of love. He was enamored with an actress named Lydia Thompson. During his stay in the Crescent City, he was given the honor of selecting the official Mardi Gras colors by the Krewe of Rex. His selection of purple, green, and gold would also later become the colors of the House of Romanoff in Russia. The 1892 Rex Parade theme first gave meaning to the official Mardi Gras colors. Purple was symbolic of justice, green was symbolic of faith, and gold was symbolic of power.

We give homage to New Orleans because of one word. One word that exemplifies the idea of doing a "little something extra" in business. One word that according to Mark Twain was "worth traveling to New Orleans to get."

That word is lagniappe. Pronounced LAN-YAP, it is a creole word meaning "the gift" or "to give more." The practice originated in Louisiana in the 1840s whereby a merchant would give a customer a little something extra at the time of purchase. It is a signature personal touch by the business that creates goodwill and promotes word of mouth.

According to Webster's:

> **LAGNIAPPE** (lan'yap, lăn-yăp') Chiefly Southern Louisiana & Mississippi
>
> 1. A small gift presented by a store owner to a customer with the customer's purchase.

2. An extra or unexpected gift or benefit. Also
    called boot.[25]

As a creole word, it has both French and Spanish origins. The
Spanish word Napa comes from yapa, which means "additional gift"
in the South American Indian Quechua language. In Quechuan, it
comes from the verb yapay "to give more."

ENTER SAMUEL LANGHORNE CLEMENS

Samuel Langhorne Clemens first arrived in New Orleans on February 28, 1857. Clemens entered the city in pursuit of his dream of going to Brazil to become a wealthy trader. Instead, Clemens worked
as a pilot on Mississippi River steamboats. This time would leave its
mark on him both literally and figuratively. In 1863, as a newspaper
reporter in Nevada, Clemens first used the pen name Mark Twain.
"Mark twain" is a riverboat term for a measurement equaling two
fathoms (12 feet) in depth: mark (measure) twain (two). Twelve
feet was safe waters for a riverboat. Clemens became smitten with
the word lagniappe during his time in New Orleans. He referenced
it in his autobiography *Life on the Mississippi*:

> We picked up one excellent word—a word worth trav-
> eling to New Orleans to get; a nice limber, expressive,
> handy word—"lagniappe." They pronounce it lanny-
> yap. It is Spanish—so they said. We discovered it at
> the head of a column of odds and ends in the [Times]
> Picayune [newspaper] the first day; heard twenty peo-
> ple use it the second; inquired what it meant the third;
> adopted it and got facility in swinging it the fourth. It
> has a restricted meaning, but I think the people spread
> it out a little when they choose. It is the equivalent of
> the thirteenth roll in a baker's dozen. It is something

---

25. https://www.merriam-webster.com/dictionary/lagniappe

thrown in, gratis, for good measure. The custom originated in the Spanish quarter of the city. When a child or a servant buys something in a shop—or even the mayor or the governor, for aught I know—he finishes the operation by saying—'Give me something for lagniappe.' The shopman always responds; gives the child a bit of licorice-root, gives the servant a cheap cigar or a spool of thread, gives the governor—I don't know what he gives the governor; support, likely.[26]

DEFINING A PURPLE GOLDFISH

Purple represents "a little extra" whereas the goldfish stands for "differentiation." A Purple Goldfish is defined as any time a business purposely goes above and beyond to provide a little something extra to differentiate the experience and honor the relationship. It's a marketing investment back into your customer base. It's that unexpected surprise that's thrown in for good measure to achieve product differentiation, drive retention, and promote word of mouth.

SO, IS IT JUST A BAKER'S DOZEN?

Is a Purple Goldfish just like a baker's dozen? Buy a dozen donuts or bagels and get the thirteenth for free? In order to understand the reasoning behind a baker's dozen, we need to travel back to its origin in England. The concept dates back to the thirteenth century during the reign of Henry III. During this time, there was a perceived need for regulations controlling quality, pricing, and checking weights to avoid fraudulent activity. It was common for merchants to cheat customers. The Assize (Statute) of Bread and Ale

---

26. Twain, Mark. Life on the Mississippi. Boston: James R. Osgood & Co., 1883.

was instituted to regulate the price, weight, and quality of the bread and beer manufactured and sold in English towns and villages.[27]

Bakers who were found to have shortchanged customers could be liable for severe punishment. The worst of which was having your hand chopped off with an axe. To guard against the punishment, the baker would give 13 for the price of 12 to be certain of not being known as a cheat.

The irony is that the statute deals with weight and not quantity. The merchants created the "baker's dozen" to change perception. They understood that one of the 13 could be lost, eaten, burnt, or ruined in some way while still leaving the customer with an actual dozen. The baker wasn't doing it to honor the relationship initially. It was an act of self-preservation to protect their hands.

The problem with a baker's dozen is that it has become expected. Nowadays when we walk into a bakery and buy a dozen bagels, we expect the thirteenth on the house. Therefore, it is not a true Purple Goldfish. Now if you provided a 14th bagel as part of the dozen, that would be a Purple Goldfish.

ACTS OF KINDNESS

Another way to think of lagniappe or a Purple Goldfish is as an act of kindness or thoughtful little extras for your customers. There are three types of acts of kindness:

1. **Random Act of Kindness** – the 1.0 kind. We've all seen this before. Good deeds or unexpected acts such as paying tolls, filling parking meters, or buying gas for consumers. They are usually one-off, feel-good activations. A random act of kindness draws upon gift economy principles, giving

27. https://www.telegraph.co.uk/news/uknews/3081008/Bread-rules-abandoned-after-750-years.html

with no expectation of immediate return, except maybe for potential PR value.

2. **Branded Act of Kindness** – next level 2.0. Here the item given is usually tied closely with the brand and its positioning. It's less random, more planned, and potentially a series of activations. This has the feel of a traditional marketing campaign.

3. **Lagniappe Act of Kindness** – 3.0 stuff. Kindness is imbedded into your brand. Giving little unexpected extras (g.l.u.e.) is part of your product or service. This is rooted in the idea of "added value" to the transaction. Not a one-off or a campaign, but an everyday practice that's focused on customers of your brand. The beauty of creating a Purple Goldfish as a branded act of kindness is that there is no waste. You are giving that little extra to your current customers, and they will talk about it, giving you word of mouth credibility.

Here is a table that shows all three:

1.0 RANDOM	2.0 BRANDED	3.0 LAGNIAPPE
Unpromoted	Promoted	Unexpected / Expected
Untargeted	Prospect + Customers	Customer-Focused
One-Off	Campaign	Everyday
Opportunistic	Planned	Ingrained
Relevant to the Recipient	Relevant to the Brand	Relevant to Brand + Recipient
In the Field	Near Point-of-Purchase	At Point-of-Purchase
PR Focused	PR + Brand	PR + Brand + CX + WOM

The 3.0 version evolves the concept beyond a tactic or even a campaign to brand differentiator. It's a commitment that becomes a staple of the customer experience.

PURPLE GOLDFISH STRATEGY

Purple Goldfish Strategy is differentiation by added value. This means finding signature elements that help you stand out, improve customer experience, and drive positive word of mouth. They are little consistent extras that either add value or reduce effort for customers.

Is Purple Goldfish Strategy similar to Blue Ocean Strategy? Here's an explanation of Blue Ocean Strategy from creators W. Chan Kim and Renee Mauborgne:

> Blue Ocean Strategy is based on the simultaneous pursuit of differentiation and low cost. Its goal is not to outperform competition in the existing industry, but to create new market space or a blue ocean, thereby making the competition irrelevant. The opposite of blue ocean is red ocean. Characterized by competition and a crowded space, red ocean is bloody water.[28]

IS THERE A MIDDLE GROUND OR BETTER YET A MIDDLE OCEAN?

We believe that Purple Goldfish Strategy can fall between the Red Ocean and Blue Ocean. It may be difficult to find uncontested market space through the simultaneous pursuit of differentiation and low cost. Perhaps you can set yourself apart via differentiation through experience. Do little extras to add value or reduce effort for customers. See the table below.

---

28. https://www.blueoceanstrategy.com/what-is-blue-ocean-strategy/

RED OCEAN STRATEGY	PURPLE GOLDFISH STRATEGY	BLUE OCEAN STRATEGY
Compete in existing market space	Compete in existing market space, but stand out by giving little unexpected extras.	Create uncontested market space
Beat the competition	Differentiate yourself from the competition	Make the competition irrelevant
Exploit existing demand	Exploit current customer base to reduce attrition, drive loyalty, and promote word of mouth	Create and capture new demand
Make the value-cost trade-off	Break the transactional market economy mindset by adding value to exceed expectations	Break the value-cost trade-off
Align the whole system of a company's activities with its strategic choice of differentiation or low cost	Align the whole system of a company's activities in pursuit of differentiation through added value	Align the whole system of a company's activities in pursuit of differentiation and low cost

The goldfish represents differentiation via customer experience and purple represents the concept of added value. Now, let's look at a concept called Plussing.

CHAPTER 5

PLUSSING

"Whenever I go on a ride, I'm always thinking of what's wrong with the thing and how it can be improved."

- Walt Disney

What if there was a simple marketing concept that could move the needle toward achieving differentiation, driving retention, and stimulating word of mouth? What if your execution was 100 percent targeted, with zero waste, and given with a personalized touch?

We believe the answer to doing this lies in focusing a greater percentage of your marketing budget on the customer, not the prospect. Deal with the one that is "in hand" rather than the two "in the bush" by giving little unexpected extras. This enduring focus on the customers and their experience takes us to the happiest place on Earth.

WALT DISNEY AND EXCEEDING EXPECTATIONS

Walter Elias Disney was obsessed with improving the guest experience at Disneyland. He would drive the cast members and Imagineers crazy with his suggestions for improvement. Walt was also trying to figure out how to do a little bit more. So much so that he had his own word for these continuous improvements. Here is a superb summary of plussing by John Torre in the book *How to Be Like Walt: Capturing the Disney Magic Every Day of Your Life*:

> Normally, the word "plus" is a conjunction, but not in Walt's vocabulary. To Walt, "plus" was a verb—an action word—signifying the delivery of more than what his customers paid for or expected to receive. There are literally hundreds, if not thousands, of examples of Walt "plussing" his products. He constantly challenged his artists and Imagineers to see what was possible, and then take it a step further ... and then a step beyond that. Why did he go to the trouble of making everything better when "good enough" would have sufficed? Because for Walt, nothing less than the best

was acceptable when it bore his name and reputation, and he did whatever it took to give his guests more value than they expected to receive for their dollar.[29]

Disney historian Les Perkins wrote about an incident that took place at Disneyland during the early years of the park. In 1957, Walt decided to hold a Christmas parade at the new park. The cost of building floats and hiring cast members was estimated at $350,000. When the finance team at Disney heard of the plan, they flipped out. The accountants immediately found Walt and sat him down. They pleaded with him not to spend money on an extravagant Christmas parade. Nobody would complain, they reasoned, if they dispensed with the parade because nobody would be expecting it. They were already planning on being in the park. Perkins shared how Walt's response to the accountants was classic Walt:

> That's just the point. We should do the parade precisely because no one's expecting it. Our goal at Disneyland is to always give the people more than they expect. As long as we keep surprising them, they'll keep coming back. But if they ever stop coming, it'll cost us ten times that much to get them to come back.[30]

CREATING PEAK MOMENTS

Moments matter. Little things that create delight in customer experience are important. Research shows that companies focus 80 percent of their time on fixing problems as opposed to only 20 percent on creating peak moments. Peak moments matter because they hold value according to author Chip Heath. The revenue opportunity

29. Williams, Pat. How to Be Like Walt: Capturing the Disney Magic Every Day of Your Life. Boca Raton, FL: Health Communications, Inc., 2004.

30. https://grumpymickey.org/making-disney-magic-part-two-plus-verb/

from raising peaks can be as much as nine times greater. In his words:

> It helps explain what we might call the Disney Paradox: If you were to measure your minute-by-minute happiness at a Disney theme park on a hot, crowded summer day, chances are you would have been happier for most of the day if you were sitting on your couch at home. But, in memory, the Disney visit might be a highlight of your year. Because at the park, you experienced some peak moments—the kind of moments that never come from sitting on your couch: The adrenaline rush from riding Space Mountain. Your child's beaming face when Mickey comes up and gives him a hug.[31]

Peaks can deliver tremendous ROI. In their book, *The Power of Moments*, Chip and Dan Heath share a story about visiting Southwest Airlines headquarters. They asked the team if they knew the impact of funny flight safety announcements. The team said no, but added they had the data to figure it out. It turns out that humorous safety announcements take place on 1.5 percent of all Southwest flights. The data shows that passengers on those flights flew half a flight more the following year. That additional flight represents $138 million of revenue for Southwest. If they were able to increase that percentage from 1.5 to 3 percent, that would drive an additional $138 million of revenue for Southwest. Sometimes little things can make a big difference.[32]

31. https://www.forbes.com/sites/micahsolomon/2017/11/01/
    blockbuster-bestselling-authors-chip-and-dan-heath-explain-the-power-of-moments/
32. Heath, Chip, and Dan Heath. The Power of Moments: Why Certain Experiences Have Extraordinary Impact, New York: Simon & Schuster, 2017.

CHAPTER 6

POWERED BY GIFT ECONOMY PRINCIPLES

"There are two types of economies. In a commodity (or exchange) economy, status is accorded to those who have the most. In a gift economy, status is accorded to those who give the most to others."

- Lewis Hyde

An experiment was conducted in a restaurant to determine the effects of doing a little extra. The extras included a small gift and a greeting upon entry to the restaurant. Two types of gifts were used. Customers received either a small sample of yogurt or an inexpensive key chain. The experiment by Hershey H. Friedman and Ahmed Rahman aimed to study the impact of greetings and gifting on how much was spent, on the performance rating, and on how strongly the establishment would be recommended.

The experiment studied four groups:

1. Control Group - These customers received neither greeting nor gift.

2. Greeting Group - These customers received a greeting but not a gift.

3. Gifting Group - These customers received a yogurt sample or key chain but not a greeting.

4. Greeting and Gifting Group - These customers received both a gift and a greeting upon entering the restaurant.

Contrary to the Southwest example where we looked at the impact on subsequent purchases, the greeting and gifting experiment took place before the purchase. The study could measure the impact on same day sales. What was the impact? Here are the eye-opening results:

1. **The Control Group** average purchase was $7.11 (These customers received neither a greeting nor a gift.)

2. **The Greeting Group** average purchase was $8.39 (These customers received a greeting but not a gift.)

3. **The Gifting Group** average purchase was $9.39 (These customers received a yogurt sample or key chain but not a greeting.)

4. **The Greeting and Gifting Group** average purchase was $10.41 (These customers received both a gift and a greeting upon entering the restaurant.)

The difference in the amount spent between the group that was not greeted or given a gift ($7.11) and the group that was greeted and given a gift ($10.41) was a 46.4 percent increase, a considerable amount.

It is important to note that the greeting and the gifting wasn't over the top. Guests were greeted with, "Thank you for choosing [name of restaurant]. Here is a token of our appreciation." Then they were presented with their gift. The gifts were basic. The key chain was a generic branded product that is not sold or advertised by the restaurant and retailed for about 40-50 cents each. The yogurt samples were the same Dannon Light and Fit yogurt cups advertised and sold by the restaurant and retailed for about 50 cents.[33]

The study reinforces the power of a Purple Goldfish based on the underlying principle of reciprocity. Robert Cialdini shared the concept in his book, *Influence*, when he wrote, "Reciprocity is based on the idea that people who receive a gift or benefit from someone have the need to give something back in return; there is actually a feeling of indebtedness on the part of the recipient." This surplus creates an obligation and implicit expectation of return.

The conclusions in the *International Journal of Marketing Studies* are very interesting:

---

33. https://www.researchgate.net/publication/268381728_Gifts-Upon-Entry_and_Appreciatory_Comments_Reciprocity_Effects_in_Retailing

This study demonstrates that there is value in greeting customers who enter a store. Customers who are not greeted will spend considerably less, will rate the store lower on performance, and will also be less likely to recommend the establishment. Providing a small gift upon entry into a store will have an impact on how much is spent, on the performance rating, and on how strongly the establishment will be recommended. The value of a satisfied customer to a business is immense. One study showed that customers who are totally satisfied contribute 17 times more sales to a firm than customers who are somewhat dissatisfied and 2.6 times as much sales as customers who are somewhat satisfied (Whalley and Headon, 2001). If all it takes to improve attitudes of customers is an appreciatory comment and an occasional gift, then organizations should use this approach as part of their marketing communications strategies.

EXPLORING THE IDEAS OF SURPLUS AND STATUS

There is a concept in the social sciences called a gift economy. We believe it is important to the concept and reasoning behind creating a Purple Goldfish.

So, what is a gift economy? A gift economy (or gift culture) is a concept where valuable goods and services are regularly given without any explicit agreement for immediate or future rewards. Ideally, simultaneous or recurring giving serves to circulate and redistribute valuables within the community.

A gift economy is the opposite of a market economy. In a market economy, there is an exact exchange of values. The Latin for this is quid pro quo. This doesn't mean that gift economies and market economies are incompatible. According to author Kevin von Duu-glass-ittu, "In fact, many if not most of our business exchanges are grounded in Gift-based relationships whose 'gift' nature we simply are unconscious of and just assume. If you develop a keen eye for the gift-giving environment and think about all the things that gift-giving in those environments signal, 1. a surplus others want to attach themselves to, 2. a magnanimous respect for the relationship beyond all else, 3. a debt structure that is positive ..." then we must ask ourselves if it is possible to leverage the benefits of both a gift economy and a market economy.

CAN PURPLE GOLDFISH LIVE IN THE MIDDLE?

It is our contention that there is a hybrid option that can sit between the gift economy and a market economy. We call it the lagniappe economy. Let's examine the concepts of *surplus, respect,* and *positive* through the lens of a lagniappe economy:

1. **Surplus** – The idea of surplus is grounded in giving extra or creating an inequality. As we have mentioned, la-gniappe comes from the Spanish "la napa" or the Quechan "yapay" both meaning "something that is added."

2. **Respect** – The gift or little extra is about the respect for the relationship. It becomes a beacon, a sign that shows you care. It's a physical sign of goodwill and customer appreciation—a little extra beyond the transaction to honor the relationship.

3. **Positive** – A debt structure that is positive. This speaks to exceeding expectations by giving extra. The idea of an equal exchange (market exchange) is a myth in marketing. You either exceed or fall short of customer expectations. Providing that extra value creates an inequality that is

positive. The positive effect leads to a sort of indebtedness or reciprocity from the customer.

THE BENEFIT OF SURPLUS IS STATUS

As a business, why would you want to incorporate gift economy principles into your market exchanges? We believe there are three distinct reasons and corresponding benefits of the status gained by delivering Purple Goldfish:

1. **Positioning** – Stand out from your competition. If everyone is providing x, the fact that you provide x + y (gift) differentiates your offering. Less than 30 percent of customers buy mainly on price. Competing on price is a race to the bottom. You want to tap into the more than 70 percent of customers who are looking for value and a strong customer experience. ***Benefit: Differentiation***

2. **Loyalty** – Giving the little extra (gift) enhances the customer experience. It creates a bond between the business and the customer. The benefits of that bond include increased loyalty and ultimately patronage as a form of repayment. ***Benefit: Retention***

3. **Reciprocity** – Part of giving extra is to create goodwill (inequality). That inequality is repaid by positive word of mouth, spoken or digital. The best form of marketing is positive word of mouth. By giving a signature extra (gift) you provide something for your customers to talk, tweet, blog, Yelp, or Facebook about. ***Benefit: Referrals***

THE ENGINE BEHIND WORD OF MOUTH - THE V4 PRINCIPLE

Ever heard of the "vouch for" or v4 principle? We first came across the concept of the v4 principle nearly 20 years ago. Here's the sanitized version of the hilarious forum post at Sportbikes.net:

> Think about your entire history of relationships ... every person you dated long term, short term, prison term, and every random hook-up in between. The vast majority of those relationships were with someone you met through a common friend. Very rarely do you find a couple who met randomly at a bar. Most couples met through a friend, a friend of a friend, or a relative. The reason most relationships begin this way is what I call the "v4 Principle." "v4" is short for "Vouch For" and it is this reason that the majority of people in America hook-up.
>
> **EXAMPLE:** Say you're out on a Friday night and you see a cute brunette at the bar. You approach her, make small talk, and attempt to pick her up. To you she's a hottie with dating potential. To her you're just another one of the drunken masses out there trying to score. Now take the same situation as before, but when you see her at the bar she is talking to your best friend's girlfriend. Now when you approach you're SOMEBODY as opposed to the NOBODY you were before. The girl at the bar has a reference point for you and your best friend's girlfriend is there to vouch for you: "Oh, that's Fred. He's Mike's best friend. They work together at the law firm. He's a real sweetie, and he's soo cute when he's drunk."

See how it works? You're the same drunken dude either way, but now you're perceived as charming.

On a more serious note, v4 or "vouch for" is also how the majority of purchase decisions are made. A reference point or recommendation by a friend is the strongest factor impacting purchase intent.

According to research by Keller Fay:

> Personal experience with a product or service is the number one catalyst for recommendation, with 86% saying they recommend a brand or service based on first-hand experience. 60% of word of mouth (WOM) conversations include advice to buy, try, or consider a brand. Fewer than one in ten conversations advise avoiding a brand.[34]

It only makes sense to maximize the experience with your customer. Giving that little extra provides ammunition for your customers to relay their experiences.

THE POWER OF WORD OF MOUTH

One of the frustrations we've had with the measurement of marketing is that it is fundamentally flawed. It assumes that all impressions are created equal. There is no weight given to context and the delivery mechanism.

Let's have a look at advertising, sponsorship, PR, and word of mouth:

Advertising is a one-way dialogue that is inherently biased. It's unlikely that a company or brand is going to show you their warts. Ads are vested in trying to grab your attention via interruption.

---

34. https://e-channelnews.com/word-of-mouth-the-1-influence-on-business-buying-decisions/

They sell "blue sky" by putting the product in the best light. Let's call these impressions via advertising **V1**.

Sponsorship plays on the interests of the consumer. The company or brand aligns themselves with a second party. They are still vying for your attention, but now they are engaging you at a point of passion. Sponsorship works on the idea of affinity or attribution. Let's call these impressions via sponsorship **V2**.

Public Relations (PR) is the proactive process of managing the flow of information between the brand or company and its publics. It allows for exposure to the target audience via third party sources. Those sources are predominantly mainstream media. This third party authentication provides credibility to the message. The impressions gained at no cost through PR are much more valuable than those obtained by paid advertising. Let's call these earned PR impressions **V3**.

Word of Mouth (WOM) is the act of consumers providing information to other consumers. This is the **v4** principle in action. V4 means that the consumer is standing up for the product and giving personal assurances to its value. WOM has been around for thousands of years and remains one of the most powerful forms of promotion. It's a friend recommending a new restaurant or the latest movie. New social media tools like Facebook, LinkedIn, Twitter, Instagram, and Snapchat have elevated word of mouth to a new level. Call it WOM 2.0 or WOM on steroids. V4 reminds me of the old shampoo commercial where they start to split the screen by saying, "She tells two people, then they tell two people and then they tell two people ..." Soon the screen has hundreds of people on it. That's the magic of WOM.

You need to figure a way to get people to talk about and recommend your product. A small, unique, and unexpected touch that provides fuel to the word of mouth fire. The goal is to WOW your customer to the point that they want to share their experience. In the words of Francois Gosseaux:

> The reason why exceptional service is the new competitive differentiator is not just because it's easier for competitors to catch up product-wise, but because the news about exceptional service travels fast in the networks that matter—peer and friend networks where the buying decisions are increasingly being made. When people recommend products to friends, colleagues, and acquaintances, they do not focus on the features, functions, and benefits the way many marketers have been trained to do—they focus on the overall experience of adopting the solution, and the exceptional qualities of that "whole" offering. So if you are like most companies and operate in a market where it is really hard to differentiate based on the product alone, you've got to focus your attention on WOW service offerings.[35]

ARE YOU GIVING THEM SOMETHING TO TALK ABOUT?

What are your customers talking about after leaving your business, logging off your website, or hanging up the phone?

Are you invoking the advice of Bonnie Raitt in her most famous song, "Let's Give Them Something to Talk About"?

Specifically:

1. Who do we want talking?

---

35. http://customerthink.com/customer_experience_is_the_ultimate_differentiator/

2. What do we want them saying?

3. How can we add value?

Here is how Purple Goldfish Strategy addresses those issues:

- The best marketing is first person word of mouth—your customers.

- Control the things you can control—how you treat your existing customers.

- Deliver added value with your product or service—exceed customer expectations.

- Provide that little signature something extra—a Purple Goldfish.

Using a little artistic license (apologies Bonnie) on the song lyrics:

> *Let's give them something to talk about*

> *A little Purple Goldfish as they wander out*

> *Let's give 'em something to Tweet, Instagram, and Facebook about*

We've crowd sourced and collected over 1,100 examples of Purple Goldfish. Next, we'll share the ten types of Purple Goldfish and discuss how to add value or reduce effort for customers.

PART II

10 TYPES OF PURPLE GOLDFISH (THE WHAT)

CHAPTER 7

VALUE AND MAINTENANCE

"There are no traffic jams along the extra mile."

- Roger Staubach

ARE YOU DOING THE LITTLE THINGS FOR YOUR CUSTOMERS?

Giving Little Unexpected Extras (G.L.U.E.) shows you care. There are ten different types of Purple Goldfish. Half are based on "value" and half are based on "maintenance" according to the value / maintenance matrix:

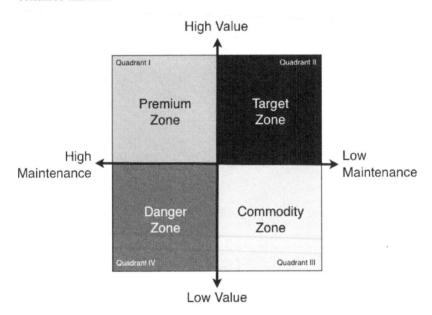

VALUE

The what and when of customer experience:

- What are the tangible and intangible benefits that your service or product provides?

- Does your product or service go above and beyond to exceed customer expectations?

- Are you giving that little unexpected extra to surprise and delight your customer?

The first five types of Purple Goldfish seek to increase value for the customer. They include:

#1. Throw-ins – little extras that are included with your product or service. They help you stand out in a sea of sameness:

> Example: "Bags Fly Free" and no change fees on Southwest.

#2. Sampling – little extras that give your customer an additional taste by offering a free something extra on the house.

> Example: Order a box of tea from Bigelow Tea and you'll be treated to a sample of another flavor on the house.

#3. Guarantees – giving your customers that little extra pledge that you'll stand behind your product or service.

> Example: Jansport backpacks are backed up ... for life.

#4. Pay it Forward – give a little extra back to the community.

> Example: If you are out of work and need a suit cleaned for an interview, Plaza Cleaners will clean it for free.

#5. First and Last Impressions – little extras that make you memorable and, more importantly, talkable. You have two chances to make an impression—when your customer comes through the "door" and right before they walk out, hang up, or log off.

> Example: Sample a Gibson guitar at Hard Rock Hotels. Check in, plug-in, and rock out.

MAINTENANCE

Maintenance focuses on the who and how of the customer experience.

- What is the buying experience like for your customer?

- Do you make things turnkey or simple for your customer?

- Are you responsive to problems / issues for your customer?

The second five types of Purple Goldfish seek to reduce maintenance for the customer. They include:

#6. Added Service – the little extra that's an added unexpected service.

> Example: Safelite repairs or replaces your auto glass, and they also vacuum your car and clean your windows.

#7. Convenience – the little extras you add to make things easier for your customers.

> Example: Most TD Bank locations are open seven days a week and some nights until 8 p.m.

#8. Waiting – the little extra to make waiting more bearable, especially if waiting is inevitable.

> Example: Pacific Cafe gives you a glass of wine on the house to enjoy while you wait for your table.

#9. Handling Mistakes – admitting that you're wrong and doing the little extra above and beyond to make it more than right.

Example: Panera corrects their mistake and then gives you a free bakery treat to apologize.

#10. Follow-up – make the little extra follow-up with your customer.

Example: Rite Aid follows up with a call to check on a patient.

HALL OF FAME EXAMPLE: ZANE'S CYCLES

Zane's Cycles is a Purple Goldfish Hall of Fame company. The company is built on customer service as a point of differentiation. A veteran of the retail bicycle industry for more than three decades, founder Chris Zane has built the Branford, Connecticut, business into one of the largest bicycle stores in the nation by giving customers more than they expect. More importantly, they stand behind the sale by giving more service than is reasonably expected (especially by competitors).

Zane's walks the talk. They are willing to spend $100 to service a customer. To illustrate the point, Chris Zane uses the metaphor of a bowl filled with 400 quarters. During presentations, he walks around with a bowl and encourages members of the audience to take quarters. Most take a few quarters, but no one ever takes the whole bowl. According to Chris:

> "The point is that when you as a customer are presented with more than what seems reasonable, like a bowl of 400 quarters, you will self-regulate. By providing more service than what folks consider reasonable, we can build trust and loyalty and remind them how hard we're working on their behalf."

Here are 10 compelling ways that Zane's offers little extras to maximize lifetime value and reduce maintenance:

1. Throw-ins (value): Gift Certificates in Water Bottles – Buy a gift certificate and Zane's will throw in a complimentary branded water bottle to hold the certificate.

2. Sampling (value): 30-Day Test Ride – Purchasing a new bike can be overwhelming, especially when many bikes feel similar. Then there are the many color options and component groups to select from at Zane's. Their goal is "to do our very best to get you on the bike of your dreams but sometimes you don't know if the bike you purchased is the right fit for you until you get out and ride. To make sure that you have purchased the correct bicycle, ride it for 30 days. If during that time you are not completely satisfied, please return the bicycle for an exchange. We will gladly give a full credit toward your new selection."

3. Guarantees (value): Lifetime Service – Every bicycle purchased from Zane's Cycles comes with their exclusive Zane's Cycles Lifetime Free Service and Parts Warranty. Anytime your bicycle needs a service, a full-tune up, or just a quick adjustment, Zane's will make those necessary adjustments for free as long as you own your bicycle.

4. Paying it Forward (value): Wishing Wheels – At the Wishing Wheels Holiday Bike Drive folks work together to assemble the many bikes that were purchased with Roots4Relief fund drive dollars over the course of five weeks. The assembled bikes then go to children in need. In 2018, Zane's was able to assemble and donate nearly 200 bikes!

5. First / Last Impressions (value): Test Rides – Want to test a bike at Zane's? You're free to take it out for a ride. No credit card or driver's license required. Each year they lose a handful of bikes, but the small cost is insignificant compared to the trust gained and hassle avoided.

6. Added Service (maintenance): Free Trade-in Program for Kids – Buy a bike for your child at Zane's. When they outgrow it, simply bring it back to trade-up. Zane's gives you a credit for the price of the former bike toward a new one.

7. Convenience (maintenance): Webcam – Zane's has a camera in the repair shop which gives customers the ability to Skype the team at work.

8. Waiting (maintenance): Coffee Bar – Zane's has a nice espresso bar in the store that encourages customers to relax and enjoy a cup of gourmet coffee while shopping.

9. Handling Mistakes (maintenance) Founder's Promise – Zane's is committed to service and getting it right. You can find this message on its website:

    "If you don't feel that we are living up to our mission, let us know and we'll fix it immediately. If you have a concern and would like to discuss it with me, Chris Zane, directly, please e-mail me. I will personally respond to you."

10. Follow-up (maintenance): Personal Notes – each person who buys a bike from Zane's receives a handwritten thank you note.

CHAPTER 8

THROW-INS FOR GOOD MEASURE

"A fellow who does things that count,
doesn't usually stop to count them."

- Variation of a saying by Albert Einstein

#1 THROW-INS

A mong the ten types of Purple Goldfish **Throw-ins** are first for two reasons. Throw-ins are the most classic form of lagniappe, as we learned from Mark Twain. Second, Throw-ins are one of the easiest types of Purple Goldfish to implement.

THROW IN THE BONUS FRIES

One of the Purple Goldfish Project Hall of Famers is Five Guys Burgers and Fries. Jerry Murrell and his five sons (literally, the Five Guys) run the business. Sons Matt and Jim travel the country visiting stores; Chad oversees training; Ben selects the franchisees; and Tyler runs the bakery. All six of them embrace the principles of Purple Goldfish, and added value is baked into the model at Five Guys. Here are a few of the things they do:

- Free peanuts when you walk through the door

- 15 free toppings for your burger or dog

- An extra handful or two of bonus fries

- Free refills for your soda or iced tea

The free peanuts you can shell are our favorite. According to Todd at cheese-burger.net:

> While you wait for your order to be prepared, there is a mountain of peanuts just inside the front door to munch on. Free peanuts have become the trademark "thing" that Five Guys is known for. I saw over fifty bags, 50 pounds apiece, waiting to be opened and devoured. They have signs at the door to serve as fair

warning for folks with peanut allergies, and they're pretty strict about not letting you take any peanuts to go as a safety precaution. But it's a pretty cool thing: order your cheeseburger, scarf down a handful of salty, ballpark-style, still-in-the-shell peanuts.

By our rough calculations, Five Guys gives away over two million pounds of peanuts per year. Do little things make a big difference? For a company that does little to no advertising, here is the mantra from founder Jerry Murrell:

> We figure our best salesman is our customer. Treat that person right, he'll walk out the door and sell for you. From the beginning, I wanted people to know that we put all our money into the food. That's why the décor is so simple—red and white tiles. We don't spend our money on décor. Or on guys in chicken suits. But we'll go overboard on food.

SOUTHWEST ELIMINATES FEES

Southwest Airlines stands for "freedom" in air travel. Following up on the successful Bags Fly Free[36] program, Southwest introduced the next chapter in eliminating fees: "No charge for change fees at Southwest. Saving customers upwards of $150."

At Southwest fees are a four-letter word, a bad four-letter word. Here is a rundown of how they treat fees:

- No checked bag fees for up to two bags

- No change fees

- No fuel surcharge fees

---

36. http://www.southwest.com/html/cs/landing/bags_flyfree.html

- No snack fees

- No aisle or window seat fees

- No curbside check in fees

- No phone reservation fees

Sometimes a Purple Goldfish is not about what you give, but rather what you decide not to charge for.

A JELLY BEAN WITH A PURPOSE AT WILSON'S ICE CREAM

Jody Padar shared this unique example with us. In her words:

> At my favorite ice cream store in Door County, Wisconsin, they put a jelly bean at the bottom of the ice cream cone so it doesn't drip. They also give the biggest scoop ever. It's tradition. The girls who scoop the ice cream live upstairs. There is never a night in the summer where the line is short and everyone happily stands on the porch waiting. They were featured on the Travel Channel and were sold recently for a few million dollars. Not bad for an ice cream store.

CHOWDER AT THE TURN

Myrtle Beach may be paradise if you are a fan of playing golf. It has roughly 125 courses within a 25-mile radius. With so many choices, how do you stand out in the "sea of sameness" as a local golf course? Enter Caledonia Golf & Fish Club on Pawleys Island, South Carolina. Built in 1995, Caledonia has earned a top billing.

In Jeff Day's words, "Caledonia Golf & Fish Club offers a cup of chowder at the turn, which is cooked and served right in front of you on the tenth tee—it's a unique experience. In addition, on Thursdays the course hosts a collegial public fish fry on the grounds for players to relax, eat, mingle, and share glowing reviews of their day."

VIVA LAS FRENCH FRIES

We learned about this Purple Goldfish at Mandalay Bay's Stripsteak from a restaurant review in the *Las Vegas Review Journal*:

> If you're even slightly tuned-in, you're no doubt aware that Michael Mina is widely regarded for his skills as a chef, most notably with fish and seafood. But you may not know that he absolutely rocks French fries and onion rings. No lie, French fries and onion rings, two of the standouts of our recent dinner at Stripsteak at Mandalay Bay. The skillful preparation of them proved why these two simple things—often deservedly scorned—have solid footholds in the culinary landscape. The French fries were a lagniappe, served shortly after we ordered our wine. Fried in duck fat, they had an extreme crispness that sharpened the contrast to their fluffy interiors. They were served as a trio (a favorite Mina conceit) with one portion dusted with smoked paprika and served with barbecue sauce, one served with aioli, the other with homemade ketchup. Servers at Stripsteak point out that entrees are served a la carte, but with a lagniappe as generous as this, that point is easy to argue.[37]

37. http://www.lvrj.com/neon/stripsteak-s-careful-preparation-shows-even-simple-things-perfectly-   prepared-112707359. html?ref=359

A FREE PIZZA AND MAKE IT SNAPPY

Matt Sheehan recommends the Alligator Lounge in Brooklyn, a place where the pizza is always on the house. Here is a snippet from *NY Magazine's* Karen Hudes on the Lounge:[38]

> Inside what was once the Galleria pizza place, this bar's turquoise walls, pink flamingos and Romanesque details don't quite gel, yet one crucial feature remains intact: the arched, wood-burning oven. Because of the owners' sensational idea of serving free personal pizzas every night until 3:30 a.m., this unremarkable joint has turned into a lovable hangout that's a great first or last barhop stop. Young and old Williamsburg folk congregate along the bar, in the maroon, open-angle vinyl booths, and around the green pool table. A booming jukebox and Big Buck Hunter Pro game in back provide entertainment. A selection of 10 draft beers complements the delicious crisp-crust pies, which are on the house with every drink; toppings like pepperoni, caramelized onions and flavorful sweet sausage are available for an extra $2.

How does the free pizza resonate with customers? Quite well. Here's a review we found from a customer:

> I don't want the place to get so crowded that I can't get in. This is a fantastic place, with Widmer Hefeweizen on tap, and of course ... free pizza. I didn't know about the pizza when I wandered in mid-week. When the bartender told me about it, I pictured pizza pockets ... but it's wonderful wood-oven, thin-crust pizza. You pay two bucks for your first topping and one buck after that. I had mine loaded, so it set me back a whole

---

38. http://nymag.com/listings/bar/alligator_lounge/

five bucks. The same pizza in Manhattan would have set me back 15 bucks. Would I be back? I'm thinking of getting an apartment above the place!

BANK OR CAFÉ?

Long before Capital One's recent Capital One Café concept, Portland, Oregon-based Umpqua Bank understood how to take banking beyond the transactions. Featured in Joseph Jaffe's *Flip the Funnel*, Umpqua adds value in little ways. Tellers place the customer's cash on a black wooden tray along with a silver chocolate coin embellished with the bank's logo. The bank has free Wi-Fi and their own brand of house coffee. And if you have an issue, there's a telephone in each branch that's a direct line to the CEO's office.[39]

KLM DELFT BLUE HOUSES

This classic Purple Goldfish was borderline illegal when KLM rolled it out in the 1950s. We first learned about it from a short email from Gene Willis: "KLM gives Delft Blue Houses to customers who fly business class."

With a little research, we learned the backstory on the houses, courtesy of Theo Kiewiet:

> The KLM houses are presents to travelers aboard KLM flights in Business and Royal Class. They have been presented over a long period and thus have become collector items. There are currently over 90 different types which are each individually numbered in order of release.

---

39. http://www.flipthefunnelnow.com/

There is Dutch Genever [gin], 35% alcohol, in the houses, which are in fact bottles with a cork and seal on top. Sometimes the genever has been drunk but mostly the empty bottles were empty all along. On flights to some countries with strict alcohol restrictions empty houses are presented. On some of the houses a sticker explains this by referring to customs regulations. Sometimes there is a cork and seal and sometimes there isn't (and never was) on the empty bottles.

KLM started issuing these miniature bottles in 1952. Airlines were not allowed to give presents to their customers because of unfair competition. So, KLM had some Blue Delft houses made and filled them with genever (gin). Then, of course, their competitors complained, "KLM is giving presents to their customers." KLM said, "May we decide how we serve our drinks? Is there [sic] a law which tells me drinks have to be served in a glass?"... and so it all started.[40]

MAGIC POPSICLES BY THE POOL

When was the last time you had a popsicle? Probably not recently. When was the last time you had a popsicle at a hotel? You probably haven't. When was the last time you had a popsicle delivered to you at a hotel? Likely never. Have you ever complained because popsicles weren't on the room service menu? Probably not.

So why would a hotel create a popsicle hotline and why would anyone care? In their book, *The Power of Moments*,[41] the Heath brothers categorize the popsicle hotline as a "peak" moment. They argue that

---

40. http://www.t-shirtforums.com/general-t-shirt-selling-discussion/t21752-12.html
41. http://heathbrothers.com/the-power-of-moments/

people value and remember small, unusual moments [micro-weird] more than larger, seemingly more important, services.

This seems to be true for the Magic Castle Hotel. They are the highest-rated hotel in the Los Angeles area according to TripAdvisor. Out of over 3,000 reviews on TripAdvisor, 94% of guests rate the hotel as either excellent or very good.[42]

But why are the ratings so high? Wouldn't people rather stay at a consistently luxurious property like the Four Seasons? The Magic Castle Hotel doesn't have an amazing pool or beautiful furniture or lovely rooms. It doesn't have most of the things that you'd expect from a great hotel. What it does have is a Popsicle Hotline.

Here's how it works. There's a red phone on a wall by the pool. When you lift the handset, a popsicle specialist answers and takes your order. You don't have to wait long before an employee wearing white gloves brings your popsicles on a silver tray at no charge.

As the Heath brothers explain:

> What the Magic Castle has figured out is that, to delight customers, you need not obsess over every detail. Customers will forgive small swimming pools and underwhelming room décor, as long as you deliver some magical peak moments. The surprise about great service experiences is that they are mostly forgettable.

ALL IN THE DESIGN AND DETAILS

We first learned about Johnny Cupcakes from a tweet by David Knies. It turns out that Johnny Cupcakes spends time creating a few

---

42. https://www.tripadvisor.com/Hotel_Review-g32655-d84502-Reviews-Magic_Castle_Hotel-Los_Angeles_California.html

Purple Goldfish to accompany his mail order shipments. Here is a comment from a forum:

> "What a great display. So, there was a. the box, b. the tissue paper, c. the bag, d. the shirt, e. the hang tag, f. the oven mitt label, g. the home alone card, h. the business card, i. the button, and j. the candy."

Wait a second … no cupcakes? Turns out that Cupcakes is Johnny's nickname. His last name is really Earle and Johnny Earle doesn't make cupcakes. He makes T-shirts and Johnny knows marketing.

Here are three marketing takeaways from Johnny Cupcakes:

1. Details, details, details – Johnny understands that you need to do the little things to stand out in a sea of sameness.

2. You need to create an experience for your customers and make your brand talkable. His products are displayed in ovens and bakery counters, the hang tags are clever, the label is shaped like an oven mitt, the product is delivered in takeout-style boxes, and the T-shirts are 80s-style designs. Together they all play a part in creating the Johnny Cupcakes brand.

3. Keep it fresh and limited – Despite numerous offers by department and specialty stores, Johnny prefers to keep it personal and only sells his products online or in his "bakery" store. All of his shirts are limited editions, some of which are runs of 100 or less.

4. Be approachable and take care of your fans – Part of Johnny's appeal is his personal story of a scrappy kid selling T-shirts out of an '86 Toyota. He's an American success story of following your passion. Johnny makes himself

accessible by blogging, releasing videos, and even hosting customer appreciation events.

MINTY FRESH AND PACKED WITH DETAIL

Joe Bob Hester, a professor at UNC-Chapel Hill, turned us on to apparel brand Peter Millar. He shared a *Charlotte Observer* article by Ron Green, Jr. that profiles the company. Here's an excerpt:

> "They remember the mints."
>
> When boxes of golf shirts and shorts and other high-end menswear are shipped from the Peter Millar office and warehouse, the packing list includes mints.
>
> When customers unpack their orders, they are struck by three things: The quality of what they've ordered; each item comes out of the box in the order it's listed on the packing sheet; and, mints are included for the pleasure of it.
>
> It's a little thing, but this year when a few boxes arrived short of mints (they ran out briefly), phone calls started coming.
>
> At Peter Millar, located in a low-profile office park on the southwest edge of Raleigh, the attention to detail, commitment to quality, and a North Carolina-grown appreciation of classic menswear has helped catapult the company into one of the hottest brands on the market, particularly for golfers.[43]

---

43. http://www.charlotteobserver.com/

ADOPT A FINGER PUPPET

One of the fun parts of the Purple Goldfish Project was seeing so many people look for Purple Goldfish from the companies they know and love. Ariel Savrin-Jacobs blogged about the project[44] and shared this story of a little added value from PerpetualKid.com:

> Last week I bought a few fun things online for my dorm room from PerpetualKid.com. It was my first time buying from them, and I'll certainly be a repeat customer. The site is overall really fun (for example, I got measuring cups that stack like a Russian nesting doll), and it definitely didn't hurt that my order placed at 10:00 p.m. on the 18th, shipped the next morning and arrived on the 20th. But the best part of it all was the surprise "finger monster" (for lack of better words) sitting on top when I opened the package. While I don't quite know what to do with it, I sure got a kick out of it, and I bet many other customers probably did too.

DON'T FORGET THE SAUCE

Long Island Legend, Maroni Cuisine sounds like a great place to eat. Their reviews tout a fixed tasting menu and legendary meatballs, but the Purple Goldfish comes at the end of the meal. Clark Johnson shared this example with us:

> Maroni Cuisine in Northport, NY is consistently rated by Zagat voters as either the best or among the best restaurants on Long Island. Mike Maroni beat Bobby Flay in a throwdown! The meals are exclusively customized tasting menus, prix fixe, with all the wine you

can drink included. At the end of the meal, hours later, guests are generally presented with jars of Maroni Pasta sauce as a "Thank You." Once you have used it, you want to go back for more (both the meal and the sauce)!

TAKE HOME SOME PASTA

A simple, but effective, Purple Goldfish comes from Italian chain, Maggiano's. They call it "Today and Tomorrow." When you buy a pasta dish, they'll pack up one for you to take home for free.

PURPLE GOLDFISH PLAY TENNIS, TOO

Will Prest of Minneapolis introduced us to Michael Lynne's Tennis Shop. Here's what he had to say:

> "When you pick up your professionally strung racquet, you get a new can of Penn balls with the Michael Lynne Tennis logo and name in big letters on it. It is a nice gesture, plus his balls are left all over the clubs around town. Here is the website.[45] It got me to visit the site and I read a few of the articles on there ... they were a nice surprise."

Companies that really get the concept of Purple Goldfish tend to have multiple examples in their arsenal. Maybe it has something to do with fish wanting to swim in schools. Here is an excerpt from an article about Michael Lynne in a tennis industry publication:

> It's not only about sales. Fully supportive of Minneapolis' large tennis community, Lynne puts kids' and local team photos on his back wall along with local

---

45. http://www.mltennis.com/

tennis stories and news. And he's happy to offer tennis tips to his customers and encourages them to "test drive" racquets for free.

Clothing is grouped by size and the price is always visible. Racks are never overcrowded and pieces are displayed on the wall so customers can see them as "outfits." When customers try on clothes, they find large dressing rooms with excellent lighting. Also, all the employees don various tennis outfits to work so customers can see what the clothes actually look like "on."

The store also has six stringing machines, so, as Michael notes, "You can have your racquets strung while you wait." But even "waiting" at Michael Lynne's Tennis Shop is a pleasure. Customers can watch the Tennis Channel on TV while having a snack or sipping gourmet coffee the shop supplies.

"We're a destination point," Lynne says. "People have to drive here, so we want to make sure our staff is well-informed on the merchandise and offers great customer service."

"Michael and Mimzy personify customer service, and they teach their staff to take this approach," says Greg Mason, senior director of sales for HEAD. "It's the little things like greeting each customer, then thanking them as they leave, writing thank-you notes to repeat customers—that really makes the difference."

The staff is always upbeat and motivated. "It's apparent they get it," says Mason. "The Minneapolis tennis market is the real winner."

Let's count the Purple Goldfish at Michael Lynne's:

- Free tennis balls with racquet restringing

- Free racquet demos

- Stringing while you wait in style

- Large, well-lit dressing rooms

- Handwritten thank you notes.

The second to last paragraph of the article says it best, "It's the little things ... that make the biggest difference."

CALL ME

Our last example of a Throw-in adds value in a fun and unpredictable way. Submitted via e-mail, Vanessa Khedouri tells us how Rebecca Minkoff adds a little extra:

> Rebecca Minkoff bags all have an extra business card in them—it has a guy's picture and on the back there is a handwritten note that says "call me," signed by "Vincent" with a phone number. When you call (+1 646 420 1475), there is a recording of a message from "Vincent"—a guy with a sexy French accent—who references his friend, "Rebecca" (the designer) and her website. I love that touch and it feels personal!

Here's the backstory according to Rebecca Minkoff:

> "I find cute pics and have them printed on cards and people actually do call! When customers call they hear a guy's voice and he is French. Some people call and

think they met the guy the night before. It's kind of funny to hear some of the messages!"

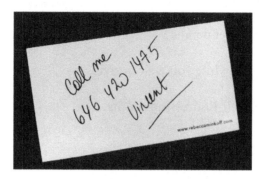

The idea of a Throw-in might sound haphazard and in-the-moment, but these brands have built their businesses on systematically including extras that are celebrated by their customers. Sometimes an extra for your customer doesn't have to be all that extra for your team.

Let's move on to the lowest hanging fruit—Sampling.

CHAPTER 9

SAMPLE THE LOWEST HANGING FRUIT

"One of the best ways to motivate consumers to try new products is through sampling. Once a consumer tries a new product through sampling, it's likely they will add it to their shopping list."

- Julie Hall

#2 SAMPLING

Sampling is the lowest hanging fruit in marketing. There may not be a more cost-effective way for brands to drive purchase intent and conversion than Sampling. The proof is in the numbers as highlighted in this Arbitron Product Sampling Study.[46] Here are the top two takeaways:

- 24 percent of consumers bought the product they sampled instead of the item they initially set out to purchase.

- 35 percent of customers who tried a sample bought the product during the same shopping trip.

But why does Sampling have to be just about the prospect? Why can't you leverage current customers with an additional little extra to increase satisfaction, drive retention, and promote word of mouth? Let's dive into some ways companies are using Sampling to delight their customers.

A LITTLE EXTRA FLAVOR

Katie Morrow shared Izzy's Ice Cream with us. For every scoop you purchase, you're given an "Izzy Scoop," which is a mini scoop of another flavor of your choice.

Izzy's Ice Cream is an ice cream store in St. Paul, Minnesota. The owner of the now-iconic shop, Jeff Sommers, was told to do two things when he opened his shop:

1. Smile

2. Give away samples

---

46. https://docuri.com/download/productsamplingstudy_59c1cab3f581710b28607af9_pdf

Jeff disliked the idea of just giving away free samples, so he created his own wrinkle—the Izzy Scoop. It's great for customers who can take a "worry free" chance to try a new flavor. It's a little extra that goes a long way, but don't take our word for it: Izzy's was voted the best ice cream shop in America by Reader's Digest.

BLUE GOLDFISH MOMENT

Izzy's was also featured in *Blue Goldfish* (our technology book) for a different reason. Izzy's has more than 150 flavors of handmade ice cream but can only keep 32 flavors in the case at any given time.

Finding a way to let the patron know when their favorite flavor was available, reducing disappointment, was a prime concern for Jeff. It was a problem he needed to solve right away. The day he found an RFID technology solution for that problem was the day revenue increased. He had solved the problem and provided added value. RFID tags identify each flavor when it is placed in the case ready to serve. The RFID system updates the inventory every 3 minutes so you can [know if] your favorite flavor is there when you are craving.

If you choose to be notified by email, you can sign up and let the system know what flavors you are looking for. There are options to be notified by Twitter updates and Facebook alerts as well. Just sign up for the updates.

Sampling, of course, isn't just limited to food and beverage operations. Many other kinds of companies have leveraged it to build loyalty too.

THIS PURPLE GOLDFISH HAS A FRAGRANT BOUQUET

Frances Lewis shared with us an example from Sephora. Here's what she had to say:

> "I was searching for a perfume for a gift, and [the] salesperson not only gave great "traditional" assistance but created customized samples in little spray containers, then bagged, and labeled them."

Frances went on to say, "I grew up in New Orleans and remember "lagniappe" very often as a tray of hard candies given in lieu of a penny's change. Great concept."

The act of creating customized samples is a nice touch and one that undoubtedly makes the purchase decision easier—even if the purchase doesn't come until days or weeks later.

KIEHL'S TRIPLES DOWN ON SAMPLING

Here's another example from the American cosmetics brand retailer, Kiehl's. According to *Real Simple* magazine, "Kiehl's hands out samples of every product it sells—approximately 10 million giveaways a year."[47]

Kiehl's offers up samples in four different ways:

- At a Kiehl's store

- At a Kiehl's counter in a department store

- Over the phone

- Online

---

47. http://beauty.thefuntimesguide.com/2007/09/kiehls_free_samples.php

What was the third one again? Call Kiehl's and tell the operator what you'd like to try and the company will send you up to three samples. If you don't believe it, here's the number +1 800 543 4572.

According to Kiehl's website:

> We understand that no two skin or hair types are exactly alike and that products work differently for each person. To ensure you find the precise products that meet your needs, Kiehl's pioneered an extensive Sampling Program many years ago. We're confident that when you try our products, you will recognize the high quality and efficacy of the preparation. We invite you to try three Kiehl's samples with your first order of the day to discover other Kiehl's formulations from our extensive line of skin, hair, and body care.

TEA TIME

Jack Campisi shared how a Purple Goldfish swam right into his tea. Well, sort of. Here's what Jack had to say:

> I found a Purple Goldfish in a box of tea today. I opened a new box of Bigelow Vanilla Chai Tea and I was surprised to see a different colored label on the tea bag I pulled out. I wondered if I had bought the wrong flavor, but it turns out it was a bonus bag of their "Constant Comment" Orange Spiced Chai Tea.
>
> It was a nice surprise and a great chance for me to sample another variety of their tea without having to buy a box of a flavor I may not like. And the good news is that I liked it.

This is a great example of lagniappe because it surprised and delighted me, and it was very relevant. If they had not done that, I probably never would have tried that kind of tea ... but now I just might go get a box. So, mission accomplished, Bigelow; you made a customer happy, turned me on to another one of your products, and you are generating word of mouth buzz. That's a Purple Goldfish.

TRY THE NONPAREILS IN-STORE

Cheryl Ahto offers up Josh Early Candies as a sweet example of a Purple Goldfish:

> Word of mouth marketing will get you into the store. Sampling their famous nonpareils will turn you into a repeat customer before you've even walked out the door. Josh Early Candies is a fifth-generation family business based in Allentown, Pennsylvania, and they understand Purple Goldfish. The quality of their candy and their friendly, hard-working sales people make for an unforgettable customer experience. But it's the Purple Goldfish—the free, incredibly delicious nonpareils that will keep you coming back for more. Believe me. I've been buying their chocolate for decades!

We have to agree. What a fantastic example. Josh Early Candies is a Lehigh Valley institution. Cheryl sent Stan a box of the nonpareils as a "thank you." There are few things in life that can live up to high expectations. Stan added Josh Early nonpareils to the list.

SMELL, SEE, TOUCH, AND TASTE IT

It is said that people don't know what they like [but] they like what they know. If you can figure out a way to make it easy and risk free, they might like something new more than what they know today.

Great Harvest Bakery has a bread of the day and allows customers to try a sample. Here's how Nicolas Nelson describes it:

> The Great Harvest Bakery is a relatively small franchise chain of wonderful American-style bakeries that is growing slowly on purpose—they want to make extra sure that every new Great Harvest Bakery is top notch and fully reflects the ethos of the original one.
>
> Lagniappe is what Great Harvest Bakery is all about—it comes across in a dozen ways. But the first one any visitor will notice immediately is the free bread tasting every time you come in the door. Yep, everyone who even stops by gets a free slice of their choice of the day's fresh-baked bread. A generous free slice.
>
> Whether or not you buy something. Whether or not you even stay in the bakery after you take their bread. Whether or not you say thank you. Free bread, every visit! Of course, there's a catch: the bread is unbelievably good. That free slice of bread will convince you to buy a whole loaf. We do, almost every week. The panini sandwiches are pretty amazing too, by the way (but not free).

TRY SOMETHING NEW WHILE YOU WAIT

We'll cover Waiting in chapter 14, but we couldn't resist sharing this example with you now. Ted Simon told us about his local Starbucks in Terra Linda, California:

> "When the line gets really long, it's common for one of the staff to come out with a tray of complimentary samples of the latest and greatest beverage. A nice treat while you wait."

We agree. The power of a Purple Goldfish kicks into high gear when you implement ideas that cross over our ten categories. Speaking of categories, we've covered the first two.

Now, let's move to the third type: Guarantees

CHAPTER 10

STANDING BEHIND YOUR PRODUCT

"Truth is that you don't know what is going to happen tomorrow. Life is a crazy ride, and nothing is guaranteed."

- Eminem

#3 GUARANTEES

The third type of Purple Goldfish involves **Guarantees**— the extra commitment that you will stand behind your product or service. In the first edition of *Purple Goldfish*, we touted LL Bean's lifetime guarantee for its products. Since publication, that guarantee has been discontinued. Not to worry, however. Many companies offer guarantees and follow through with exceptional service.

Mark Robertson caught our attention with this tweet:

> "Just received a notice from JanSport "thanking us" for returning a "vintage" backpack; they are sending us a new one free"

It's more than a bag. It's a JanSport. And it offers a guarantee that carries on for the life of the backpack.

Here's a story we uncovered:

> "Recently the JanSport backpack I've used for a number of years suffered "zipper disease" where it simply wouldn't stay zipped. I went to the JanSport web site and looked up their lifetime warranty information. It took me a week or so to box up and mail my backpack. JanSport sent me a postcard when they received my backpack. Last Friday, about a week after the postcard, my backpack arrived in the mail. JanSport replaced my zipper free of charge and shipped it free to Alaska! It works as good as new. If you need a backpack, buy JanSport. It's a great product backed by great service.

And yes, I've bought more than one backpack from them."[48]

The first-hand customer accounts go on and on. Another from Hillary Lipko shows how JanSport goes above and beyond:

I got my backpack back from JanSport yesterday, and I must say that I am more than impressed with the quality of the repairs. In fact, I'd say that they went well above and beyond the repairs I sent it in for. In the letter that I included with the backpack when I sent it, the only repairs I mentioned were that it needed the main compartment zipper replaced and I needed the straps replaced. The zipper had contracted the dreaded "zipper disease," and the foam in the straps had compressed so much that it might as well not have been there anymore. (Provided, these problems had occurred after about eight years of continuous use, which I think is pretty damn good.) Not only did they fix these things well beyond my satisfaction, they also replaced the handle on the top of the bag, the zipper pull that had broken off the front pocket, and the fraying of the fabric on some of the inside seams of the bag. None of those things bothered me, but I am beyond pleased that their repair center apparently takes time to assess the returned bag for everything that needs fixing rather than just relying on what the customer tells them.[49]

Guarantees can cover everything from repairs and pricing to overall satisfaction. Here are some of our favorite examples.

---

48. http://alaskanlibrarian.wordpress.com/2008/08/25/jansport-delivers/

49. http://lamenta3.disavian.net/2009/02/return-of-the-backpack/

GUARANTEED NOT TO OVERPAY

We kicked off this section of the book with Zane's Cycles, but it's worth mentioning their guarantee once more. Jeanne Bliss shared "90-Day Price Protection" with us. Here's what Zane's has to say.

> "We guarantee you will never overpay at Zane's Cycles. If you find any item you purchased in stock for less anywhere in Connecticut within 90 days, we'll gladly refund you the difference, plus an additional 10% in cash."

UFOS AND NOISY COWS

In 1989, Hampton Inn rolled out its 100% satisfaction guarantee. At every Hampton Inn, the guarantee is etched on a plaque at the check-in desk for each customer to see: "If you're not 100% satisfied, we don't expect you to pay. That's our promise and your guarantee."

The Points Guy dug up a press release[50] from the 10th anniversary of the guarantee back in 1999. Here's their summary:

> I found an interesting article published around the policy's 10-year anniversary, noting that the guarantee has been invoked for reasons both simple (rough toilet paper) and peculiar (UFO sightings and noisy cows). The article also stated that the first 10 years saw over $6 million in free rooms given away. However, a senior VP noted that the chain was able to track more than $41 million in repeat business over that same time directly connected to the guarantee.[51]

Clearly the guarantee has paid off for Hampton Inn, and we're sure it has continued to do so.

---

50. https://www.hotel-online.com/News/PressReleases1999_4th/Oct99_HamptonGuarantee.html

51. https://thepointsguy.com/2015/04/100-satisfaction-guarantees-at-hotels-fact-or-fiction/

365-DAY GUARANTEE AND A QUIRKY EXCEPTION

Zappos is a classic customer experience example because you can credit its success in large part to the customer experience. Their guarantee, a 365-day return policy, is rare in retail. Here's how they word it:

> If you are not 100% satisfied with your purchase from Zappos you can return your item(s) for a full refund within 365 days of purchase.[52]

While the extra time is helpful to customers, the policy also demonstrates that Zappos wants a long-term relationship with its customers. They further demonstrate this desire with their refund policy for Rewards Members:

> Rewards Members—WE'VE GOT GOOD NEWS! Gold, Platinum, and Elite Zappos Rewards members enjoy instant refunds! From the first scan at UPS—we'll issue your refund, so you can skip the 5-10 Business Days.

And here's the quirky part, if you make your purchase on Leap Day—that's February 29 which comes around every four years—you'll have until the next February 29 to make your return. That's 1,461 days to return your product.[53]

CAR BUYING WITHOUT THE PRESSURE

Buying a used car is a stressful experience, even when you can see and drive the car. Online-only used car sellers tend to have generous return provisions to make you feel comfortable. For example, Carvana has a 7-day, no questions asked guarantee.

---

52. https://www.zappos.com/general-questions#return

53. https://www.businessinsider.com/zapposcom-is-celebrating-leap-year-by-quadrupling-its-return-policy-2012-2

Beyond the guarantee, Carvana goes out of their way to make the buying process convenient. They offer free delivery of your new car via a flatbed truck.

PINK GOLDFISH MOMENT

Pink Goldfish covers ways that companies achieve competitive separation by deviating from expectations. Carvana also has a Pink Goldfish trick up its sleeve. It's a car vending machine.

Stan and Evan first saw the Carvana Vending Machine along I-40 in Nashville, Tennessee, in 2016. If you choose, you can have your car delivered via an elevator and conveyor belt from a five-story machine. There's even an over-sized coin for you to drop in the coin slot!

Guarantees reduce pressure. Guarantees allow you to take chances without taking risks.

Humans tend to avoid pain rather than seek pleasure. Guarantees allow you to leverage this human behavior of avoiding pain to your advantage and the customer's too. Guarantees are just good business.

CHAPTER 11

PAYING IT FORWARD

"One of the deep secrets of life is that all that is really worth doing is what we do for others."

- Lewis Carroll

#4 - PAYING IT FORWARD

Sometimes the little extra is not about the customer but rather about giving back to the community or to those in need.

HOME AWAY FROM HOME

On our first cross-country speaking tour, we learned about Extended Stay America's Hotel Keys of Hope program. The program offers deeply-discounted and even free hotel rooms for cancer patients who must travel for treatment. Here's how the American Cancer Society describes the program:

> Getting the best care sometimes means cancer patients must travel away from home. This can place an emotional and financial burden on patients and caregivers during an already challenging time. Extended Stay America, a leading extended stay hotel chain, has committed to making this difficult situation easier for cancer patients and their families.
>
> With a passion to support a charitable cause so close to the hearts of its employees, in 2013 Extended Stay America partnered with the American Cancer Society Hope Lodge® to create the Hotel Keys of Hope program, which provides free and deeply discounted hotel stays for cancer patients in need of potentially lifesaving treatment away from home. Extended Stay America hotels provide a unique, home-away-from-home for cancer patients receiving treatment [with] amenities like fully equipped kitchens, free in-room Wi-Fi, on-site laundry facilities and pet-friendly room options, [allowing] patients to lodge with their caregivers, children, and even beloved pets to provide healing. In-room kitchens allow guests to maintain

their dietary routines and also save money by avoiding restaurant costs. Here is the impact of the program:

- Since 2013, Extended Stay America has provided 120,000 hotel room nights to cancer patients [who were] undergoing treatment away from home.

- The Hotel Keys of Hope program has helped 15,000 cancer patients receive access to potentially lifesaving cancer treatments.

- The program has helped cancer patients and their families save $7,000,000 in hotel expenses to ease their financial stress.

"The Hotel Keys of Hope program literally saved my life. After six months, I was so tired of living out of my car, staying at friends' houses, asking for favors, while in cancer treatment five days a week. I was at my wit's end and prayed, dear God, please provide me somewhere to stay, I can't do this any longer. So when I learned about Extended Stay America's lodging program in partnership with the American Cancer Society, I knew my prayers were answered." - Hotel Guest & Cancer Survivor[54]

We believe everyone can agree that paying it forward isn't just good business, it's also good for business.

---

54. https://www.cancer.org/our-partners/extended-stay-america.html

CLEAN SUITS FROM THE HEART

Blue Young shared with us this example from Plaza Cleaners in Portland, Oregon:

> "I think it counts, though it's not so typical. They will clean someone's suit for free if they're unemployed and need the suit for a job interview."

We like this example because it's simple, related to the business's core service, and helps people in a unique way.

HONORING THE TROOPS

Ryan Macaulay let us know about Coffee Bean & Tea Leaf's program to support troops overseas. In Ryan's words:

> "At Coffee Bean & Tea Leaf in LA, if you buy a bag of coffee to support our troops overseas, Coffee Bean will buy your round of coffee at the time of purchase. Even better, there is a blank white area on the actual coffee bag designated specifically for you to write a personal message to the troops the coffee is going to!"[55]

SAVE MONEY AND PLANT TREES

Chegg, the textbook rental company, has a unique Purple Goldfish related to its core mission. Here's how Gaspedal describes it:

> College students love Chegg for their cheap textbook rentals, free shipping, and eco-friendly business philosophy. Chegg believes that renting a book instead of buying it new helps save trees. This isn't just their

---

55. http://www.qsrmagazine.com/news/coffee-bean-tea-leaf-run-promotion-troops

corporate mission statement; the company actually functions around this core value. For every book they rent, they plant a tree in return. As the customer finishes their transaction, Chegg presents a world map and asks the customer to pick a country or region to plant their tree in. It's a simple, visual way of engaging during the transaction process and giving back to the community at the same time. Customers can then tell the world what they did by linking their Chegg transaction to their Facebook profile or Twitter account.[56]

ONE FOR ONE

TOMS believes in the power to improve people's lives through business. The company was founded on a model that matched every pair of shoes purchased with a new pair of shoes for a child in need. The program is called "One for One®." TOMS has given over 70 million pairs of shoes to children in need. The shoes are always given to children through humanitarian organizations who incorporate shoes into their community development programs. The One for One concept has spread from shoes. TOMS Eyewear was launched in 2011 and has helped restore sight to over 400,000 people in need. TOMS Roasting Co. launched in 2014 and has helped provide over 335,000 weeks of safe water in 6 countries. With each purchase of TOMS Roasting Co. Coffee, Giving Partners provides 140 liters of safe water (a one-week supply) to a person in need. In 2015, TOMS Bag Collection was founded with the mission to help provide training for skilled birth attendants and to distribute birth kits containing items that help a woman safely deliver her baby. As of 2016, TOMS has supported safe birth services for over 25,000 mothers. TOMS purpose "to use business to improve lives" is amply

---

56. http://www.gaspedal.com/

carried out by the expanding and very effective One for One program with the buy one, give one philosophy.[57]

RED GOLDFISH MOMENT

Rather than donating the glasses outright, [Warby Parker] makes cash donations from its sales to VisionSpring, a nonprofit for which Warby Parker founder, Neil Blumenthal, used to work. VisionSpring trains low-income men and women to sell glasses in their communities for affordable prices, allowing them to earn a living. This helps ensure Warby Parker's donations actually meet people's needs and don't displace local businesses. As of 2015, Warby Parker has distributed more than 1 million pairs of glasses through 10,000 emerging market entrepreneurs. By providing cash donations to create products for sustainable jobs for low income men and women, Warby Parker's Red Goldfish Buy a Pair, Give a Pair fulfills both parts of the company's purpose: "offer designer eyewear at a revolutionary price, while leading the way for socially conscious businesses."[58]

---

57. https://www.entrepreneur.com/article/220350

58. http://www.inc.com/magazine/201505/graham-winfrey/neil-blumenthal-icons-of-entrepreneurship.html

CHAPTER 12

PRIMING THE POWER OF PRIMACY AND RECENCY

"We don't know where our first impressions come from or precisely what they mean, so we don't always appreciate their fragility."

- Malcolm Gladwell

#5 - FIRST AND LAST IMPRESSIONS

One of the foundations of Purple Goldfish is the idea of leveraging both primacy and recency. They say (whoever they are) that people tend to remember the first thing and the last thing they see. A ton of attention is paid to the importance of a first impression (primacy), but little is made of the last moment (recency). The concept of doing a little unexpected extra at the time of purchase is a recency strategy. This is partly explained by Nobel Prize Winner Daniel Kahneman as the Peak-End Rule.[59] Kahneman believes that we judge our past experiences almost entirely on how they were at their peak (whether pleasant or unpleasant) and how they ended.

According to *Forbes* columnist Dean Crutchfield:

> "Designing for the peak-end rule is another way of not focusing on what is less important, but about focusing on what brings the most value to the customer experience. In other words, make sure that your peak and end is memorable, branded and differentiated."[60]

You never get a second chance to make a first or last impression. Translation: You need give the customer something to talk about right before they leave, hang up, or log out.

THE POWER OF A CHOCOLATE CHIP COOKIE

The chocolate chip cookie has been a thread throughout the research for this book. The first submission in the Purple Goldfish Project, a quest for 1,001 examples, was from Tom Haidinger—the DoubleTree Chocolate Chip Cookie.

---

59. http://www.sundoginteractive.com/sunblog/posts/the-brand-experience-and-the-peak-end-rule
60. http://www.forbes.com/sites/deancrutchfield/2011/12/19/i-experience-therefore-i-shop/

DoubleTree, along with their signature chocolate chip cookie, was named so many times they own the distinction of being the first brand inducted into the Purple Goldfish Hall of Fame. DoubleTree has built a reputation on a treat that keeps leisure and business travelers coming back for more: its legendary chocolate chip cookie presented to each guest at check-in. Their signature DoubleTree chocolate chip cookies are baked fresh daily, providing a warm welcome and refreshing hospitality for travelers around the world.

Here are a few fun facts about the cookie:

- DoubleTree began giving out chocolate chip cookies to their guests in the early 1980s, when many hotels across the country used them as treats for VIPs.

- In 1995, DoubleTree enlisted the services of Nashville, Tennessee-based Christie Cookie Company to hold the brand's secret recipe, which ensures that the same delicious cookie is delivered consistently at every DoubleTree hotel and resort.

- Every DoubleTree chocolate chip cookie is baked fresh daily at each hotel.

- Each cookie weighs more than 2 ounces and has an average of 20 chocolate chips.

To date, more than 400,000,000 cookies have been served to delighted guests and customers. More than a million chocolate chip cookies have been donated by DoubleTree hotels to celebrate and thank deserving members of the community from doctors and nurses to police and firefighters as well as non-profit groups such as orphanages, food banks, and homeless shelters.

From the United Kingdom to Canada and Italy to China, the signature chocolate chip cookie welcome is now being presented to travelers at DoubleTree by Hilton Hotel locations around the world.

What's so special about a cookie?

DoubleTree offers an explanation right on the brown paper bag the cookie comes in. "Why a cookie?" the headline asks. "Cookies are warm, personal and inviting, much like our hotels and the staff here that serves you."

Quoted in an article by *The New York Times*, Erich Joachimsthaler, Vivaldi Partners' chief executive, shared, "When consumers don't know how to judge the benefits or the differentiation of a product—I don't know the difference between Midwest and JetBlue and United—then a meaningless attribute like cookies can create meaningful differentiation .... The giveaway creates buzz, it creates differentiation, it increases a purchase decision."

We're not sure if we agree with "meaningless," especially if that little extra is a signature element. We subscribe to the philosophy that Malcolm Gladwell offered in *The Tipping Point*, "The little things can make the biggest difference." The chocolate chip cookie is not just a chocolate chip cookie. It's much more than that.

DoubleTree isn't the only brand who gets the first impression correct.

CHECK IN AND ROCK OUT

Hard Rock Hotels in Chicago and San Diego have the "Check In. Rock Out." program for guests. Here's how Jane Engle from the *LA Times* describes it:

> Want to feel like a rock star? You don't need an agent. Just check into the Hard Rock Hotel San Diego and check out a $2,000 electric guitar.
>
> On the heels of Hard Rock Hotel Chicago, which began the "Check In. Rock Out." program more than a year ago, the San Diego link in the music-themed chain is letting guests use handmade, high-end Gibson guitars for free. Among the models are Les Paul Studios, SG Standards and SG Specials according to Blake Smith, global music marketing manager for Hard Rock International. Besides the instrument, you get amps and headphones so that you don't disturb other guests.
>
> And please, please don't trash the room. Because you're not really a rock star, are you?[61]

The Hard Rock Hotel has another positive impression. This time a last one right before bed. At the Universal Studios Orlando location, you might find a unique gift on your pillow. From a post by Lou Imbriano:

> "Another fun amenity of staying at the Hard Rock Hotel at Universal is that instead of finding mints left on your pillow each night before bed, you discover guitar picks, funky bracelets, or smiley faced super balls, giving a new meaning to "have a nice day."[62]

A SPECIAL FIRST IMPRESSION

In Tacoma, Washington, the Hotel Murano went above and beyond for Brian Forth. Here's how Mark Brooks described his friend's hotel experience on LostRemote.com:

---

61. https://www.latimes.com/travel/la-xpm-2011-feb-02-la-trb-hard-rock-gibson-20110201-story.html

62. http://www.louimbriano.com/2011/03/24/its-universal-theyre-trying-harder/

Brian Forth recently made a reservation at the Hotel Murano in Tacoma, Washington. After making the reservation, Brian tweeted about how he was looking forward to having a stay-cation with his wife in honor of his birthday. When the couple entered the hotel, they were greeted by name and given an automatic upgrade at no charge. When they entered the room, they found a welcome package including gourmet cupcakes. Naturally, Brian tweeted some more about all the nice surprises.

Upon check-in, he inquired about whether the hotel shuttle would ferry [him] and his wife to a local steakhouse for dinner. Later, he posted the same question on Twitter. About three minutes afterward, the phone rang in his room and the concierge informed him that the shuttle would be available whenever it was needed.

So, Brian tweeted again. And the culmination of those tweets, from [Brian] a respected local business owner, had arguably more marketing power than any local advertisement the hotel could have purchased with the money they spent making Brian and his wife happy. Think about it: the cupcakes cost $5, the rest of it was just awareness and hustle.[63]

Mark talked about how the Hotel Murano was voted #6 on the Condé Nast Traveler's Reader's Choice list.[64] He went on further to state that this distinction has puzzled many of the locals, especially those in Seattle. So—how do they do it?

The proof is in the pudding ... or maybe in the cupcakes. The companies who understand Purple Goldfish tend to get the little things

63. http://www.lostremote.com/2010/01/15/social-media-powers-local-word-of-mouth-marketing/

64. http://www.exit133.com/5551/hotel-murano-6-in-conde-nast-readers

right. Whether it's greeting a first-time customer by name (they probably had Brian's picture from his Twitter profile) to a complimentary room upgrade or a shuttle ride—the Hotel Murano gets it.

By the way, in case you feel you might be missing out on those miles or points, just whip out another hotel loyalty card and the Hotel Murano will hook you up with some immediate swag.

WHAT'S YOUR COLD DRINK?

When you're having a bad day, a good first impression can mean the world to you. We learned about Mountain View Tire from a Business Voice post. Here's the post:

> One of our many great clients is Mountain View Tire, a 29-store tire and automotive service company in southern California. The other day I was adding testimonials to the new website we just built for them when I saw this one:
>
> "I wanted to make it known that I received exceptional service beyond anything I could have ever expected from your [store] in Burbank, California.
>
> I was heading to Lebec, California, and blew out my tire just north of Burbank. I called the Magnolia [Road] location and spoke with Leville Slayton. He dispatched Jacob Pomaville to my location where he retrieved the tire from my vehicle, brought it back to the store, replaced the tire, and repaired the wheel.
>
> Amid this stressful situation, Jacob had a cold drink ready for me and, beyond that, actually purchased two

jack stands from a nearby auto parts store, as neither one of us had them.

I wanted to share this story with you as it is a rarity, especially in the Los Angeles area. They have secured me as a new customer with their exceptional service and care."

I know the folks at Mountain View Tire pride themselves on providing "the WOW experience" for their customers, but the fact that Jacob brought the stranded customer a cold drink just blew me away!

It shows that he was thoughtful enough to anticipate what the customer may have needed, given what he was experiencing: the flat tire, the hot sun, being stranded, the feelings of frustration! (You've probably been there. So, think how you'd feel if Jacob showed up, not only to fix your tire, but with free refreshments!) The customer needed relief, both physically and emotionally, and Jacob was intuitive enough—or trained well enough—to understand and react to those needs.

Nothing calculated. Nothing out of the Mountain View marketing plan. Just a 99-cent bottle of water or pop that secured me as a new customer. Perfect.

What about your company? How are you delivering "cold drinks" to your customers? Again, it's not something that has to be "part of the plan," but, for it to work on a sincere, memorable human level, the question "how can I best serve my customer today" needs to be part of your company's DNA. When that question permeates your culture and your staff works every day to answer it, you'll garner the type of loyalty and earn the good word of mouth that Mountain View Tire does.[65]

A SURPRISE THANK YOU

Owen Clark shared this great example from Arigato:

> In Roseville, CA, Arigato offers half-priced sushi, all the time. Started as a promotion when the place opened [it] was so successful, they never got rid of it. Even though I know it's permanent it still makes you feel like you're getting a great value every time you go in.
>
> Especially because the menu still has the full-prices and you don't really see the savings until you get the bill. Also, [the] sushi is good enough that they could be charging a lot more.

Half off every day is a distinctive pricing model. It looks like a "wink, wink" in-the-know play. You only see the discount when your bill is presented. Talk about surprise and delight for a first timer.

SPICY MAC, A TINFOIL SWAN, AND OYSTER SHOOOOOTERS!

Tucked under the Morrison Bridge in Portland, Oregon, is a restaurant that boasts a handful of Purple Goldfish. Here are three of our favorites from Le Bistro Montage:

---

65. http://www.businessvoice.com/blog/are-you-delivering-cold-drinks/

- A signature dish is Spam and Mac, macaroni and cheese with your favorite mystery canned meat. For a little lagniappe on the flavor, you can order it SPICY.

- Oyster and Mussel Shooters are slimy fellas served in a shot glass with some cocktail sauce and horseradish. Once ordered, the waiter or waitress will immediately scream to the kitchen "OYSTER SHOOOOOTER."

- Your leftovers get wrapped up in tin foil. Move over balloon animal guy, the staff at Le Bistro Montage will "WOW" you with their tin foil animals.

WELCOME TO MOE'S

If you've ever been to Moe's Southwest Grill, you know it's known for its signature welcome. The chain has grown to more than 700 restaurants nationwide. From *QSR Magazine*:

> Can a brand measure friendliness? Moe's Southwest Grill is surely trying. Over the years, Bruce Schroder, the FOCUS Brands chain's president, says Moe's off-beat persona has stood as more than just a differentiator—it's a constant point of operational emphasis. The "Welcome to Moe's!" greeting, for example, is something the 700-unit chain actually actively surveys. Currently, employees are hitting the mark about 90 percent of the time.

> "That's good news and we're proud of the fact we do it that often," Schroder says. "But that can work against us unfortunately. When customers don't hear it, they're disappointed."

The insight is invaluable, Schroder adds. In a restaurant landscape stirred by off-premises and convenience, where guests can pick up their phone and scroll through brands quicker than status updates, having a culture this compulsive is worth guarding. And it's guiding Moe's through one of the most competitive segments in quick service, even as its unit count and systemwide sales steadily climb.[66]

The quick-service restaurants segment is competitive and Moe's succeeds on the power of being friendly and offbeat. Speaking of offbeat, Moe's also earned a spot in *Pink Goldfish*.

PINK GOLDFISH MOMENT

Moe's doesn't play just any music at its stores. Instead, it uses a hand-selected playlist of songs from deceased artists—or covers of their songs—a rep said. The lineup is updated twice a year, and franchise owners can put in song requests.

DEPARTURE BEACH

Our friend Adrian Swinscoe featured Virgin Holidays in his book, *Punk CX*. Here's what he had to say about the new amenity they created:

> When Pauline Wilson started her role as Operations Director of Virgin Holidays, she went undercover with her Marketing Director on one of their own holidays, to experience it through the eyes of their customers.

---

66. https://www.qsrmagazine.com/exclusives/moes-wants-be-friendliest-brand-america

One of the biggest lightbulb moments from their trip came when their customers kept telling them how much they didn't like the last day of their holiday.

Not because they hadn't had a great holiday, but more because after they had checked out of their hotel, they were left with time to kill and little access to any facilities before heading off to the airport to catch their flight home.

Overall, they felt forgotten, and that, after they had checked out, the company had switched its focus away from them to the new arrivals.

That was a real wake-up call for Pauline and her colleague and made them realize that the finish of any experience is just as important as the start.

That insight helped them develop a new concept: The Departure Beach. This involved a dedicated Virgin Holidays beach lounge at the hotel, which aims to help their customers get the most out of the last day of their holiday.

Are you overlooking the end of your customer's experience with you?

What could you do to make the end of your customer's experience better?

Adrian summed it up best. What are you doing to improve the last experience your customer has with your brand?

The value types of Purple Goldfish are complete with first and last impressions. Now let's tackle maintenance.

CHAPTER 13

ADDING ADDED SERVICE

"It has long been an axiom of mine that the little things are infinitely the most important."

– Sir Arthur Conan Doyle

#6 - ADDED SERVICE

After covering five ways to increase value, this chapter marks the first type of maintenance-focused Purple Goldfish. **Added Service** embodies the idea that a little extra service can exceed the expectations of your customers.

THIS ONE LEAVES NO FINGERPRINTS OR DUST

Lee Silverstein submitted Safelite to the Purple Goldfish Project. He shared his blog post called "Adding Value Doesn't Have to Cost a Nickel." In short, after replacing your damaged windshield, Safelite cleans all of your windows and vacuums the interior of your car. Here's the post:

> How do you differentiate "good" service from "great" service? You know it when you experience it, but sometimes it's difficult to verbalize. I like to explain the difference as "great" service is the type of service that you would tell others about.
>
> You could walk into a store and be cheerfully greeted, but it's unlikely that over dinner that evening you would tell your family about the friendly greeting you received while shopping earlier in the day. Now if that same associate had offered to gift-wrap your purchase and then carried it out to your car for you, then that would be an experience worth sharing. So how do companies, and their employees, take the steps to "make a difference?" By adding value.
>
> Making it standard practice to call other locations to find an out-of-stock item adds value to a customer's experience. The car dealer that washes your car when you bring it in for service also adds value. And here's

the good news for these businesses: doing these "little things" costs next to nothing!

While driving the other day, a pebble hit my windshield, leaving a small crack. I contacted my insurance company, Progressive, and they offered to book an appointment for me to have the windshield replaced the following morning; I was very impressed. As promised, my phone rang shortly after 8 am. It was Rich from Safelite AutoGlass telling me he was on his way to my home to replace my windshield. After only 45 minutes he called me and asked me to meet him outside; he was finished and needed my signature. I walked outside to find him cleaning not just my windshield, but all of my windows! Not only that, but he informed me that he vacuumed the interior of my car as well. By investing 10 extra minutes to vacuum my car and clean my windows, Rich took a good experience and made it a great one. And what did this cost Safelite? Ten minutes of an employee's time; a good investment.[67]

Our friend Allison Janda shared how this experience made her feel on the day her car was broken into. In her words:

I can still recall that stomach sinking feeling that came over me when I realized my car had been broken into. There was nothing extraordinary about what happened. I hadn't left anything massively valuable in plain sight. Cars get broken into regularly. Yet, when it happens to us, our entire world is turned upside down. We think of our vehicles as these safe, indestructible shells when in reality, they're vulnerable just like we

---

67. http://www.customerthink.com/blog/safelite_repairs_safelite_replace_safelite_does_a_little_extra

are. Safelite Auto Glass not only understands this, but they seemed determined to make me feel like a VIP, with vacuum and wipe service, on a day nothing else seemed to be going right.

Getting auto glass replaced doesn't have to be a big headache. Safelite proves that with their outstanding customer service. By taking care of all the worries that surround a window replacement on a vehicle, Safelite is one giant leap ahead of their competition.

COMPLIMENTARY TONER VACUUMING

Develop a service that's convenient, good for the environment, and saves you money. Then deliver it with a couple of Purple Goldfish. That's the order of the day for the folks at Cartridge World. Here is the example submitted by EJ Kritz:

> To begin, we're in the business of refilling and re-manufacturing printer cartridges. We offer a free delivery service to our business customers during which time plenty of things can happen opening the door for added value.
>
> For example, if we're delivering a cartridge for a laser printer but the business's fax machine is on the fritz, it's only natural and fitting that we'll do anything we can to help get their fax back up and running. Similarly, many of our franchises keep a "toner vac" in their delivery vehicle. This vacuum is specially designed to handle the fine particles in toner. It's a HUGE benefit to our customers (as silly and small as it sounds) to bring in the toner vac for a complimentary cleaning of their laser printer before we put in their new cartridge. This service is the printer equivalent of getting

a free car wash each time you get a tank of gas ... it doesn't help your car run better but it sure does make you feel good.

The last example is something almost universal regardless of which Cartridge World franchise you visit. It's quite simple actually. Each and every business delivery comes complete with a Tootsie Pop. You see, purchasing our product is all about saving money. However, typically the person saving the money (the business owner) is not the same person taking the delivery (the office manager). This little token makes everyone smile in the middle of a busy day! In fact, many of our owners could even tell you the favorite flavor of pop for each of their top customers. Simple, and yes, sweet.

RECOMMENDING A COMPETITOR

We've mentioned Zappos previously, but here's another worthy example that comes from Joe Gascoigne, who cites another way Zappos goes above and beyond. In Joe's words:

> "As for an example, one that springs to mind is that if you try to order shoes from Zappos and they do not have the shoes you want in stock, they will actually recommend a nearby store that does. It seems counter-intuitive, but I think it really builds trust and it obviously works well for them."

According to an interview with CEO Tony Hsieh in *Chief Marketer*, he refuses to see customer service as an expense. Rather, it's an investment:

"Our business is based on repeat customers and word of mouth. There's a lot of value in building up our brand name and what it stands for. We view the money that we spend on customer service as marketing money that improves our brand."[68]

Here is another great example from an article in *Footwear News*:

According to Jerry Tidmore, who manages Zappos' help-desk concierge service:

"One of the craziest stories was that of a customer who checked in to the Mandalay Bay hotel [in nearby Las Vegas] and forgot her shoes." According to Tidmore, the guest called Zappos, where she had originally purchased the style, looking for a replacement, but they didn't have any in stock. So, the company found a pair in the right size at the mall, bought them and delivered them to the hotel—all for free."

The examples keep coming. Here's another way Zappos obliterated expectations for Peter Osbourne.

My son lost one of his dress shoes at school the other day. Don't ask. I don't know how you lose one shoe.

So last night (Tuesday) he and his mother went to the store where he bought them. Nothing in his size. They get home and for a variety of reasons they don't get online until about 10:00 p.m. They find the shoes and my wife calls Zappos to confirm that we'll get the shoes by Thursday with one-day shipping. I'm not clear on the rest of the conversation, but Zappos waives the

---

68. http://directmag.com/online/marketing_workers_paradise/

overnight delivery charges. No reason given, but it sounded like it was because we were first-time buyers.

It's like Tony Hsieh was sitting outside the house when we ordered Tyler's shoes. So we get up this morning to find an e-mail with a tracking number. The doorbell rings at 9 a.m. It's the UPS guy with the shoes. That's right. Eleven hours after ordering the shoes, we had them. The customer survey arrived shortly after delivery and guess how my wife filled out the score? She's now a customer for life.

Zappos has gotten a lot of great press in recent months and was purchased in July by Amazon, which says it's leaving management in place after the sale closes. Smart man, that Jeff Bezos.

As a first-time buyer, Zappos didn't just exceed our expectations. They obliterated them.[69]

Zappos located their own distribution center next to UPS in Kentucky. They staff the center 24/7/365 which guarantees orders get picked and shipped right away. This is just one of the reasons they can pull off seemingly heroic feats of delivery.

When was the last time you obliterated a customer or client's expectations? How can you "Zappos" someone's expectations the next time you deal with them?

Recommending competitors when you don't have the product, hand delivering a pair of shoes, and upgrading to overnight shipping makes Zappos a pioneer in ways to proactively add service.

---

69. http://posborne1.wordpress.com/2009/09/30/simply-great-service-zappos/

Fitting for a shoe company "powered by service" or more appropriately according to Hsieh, "a customer service company who sells shoes."

A PERSONAL TOUCH MAKES ALL THE DIFFERENCE

Jim Joseph, author of *The Experience Effect* offers an experience with Lacoste:

> I submit to you a great example of amazing customer service that transformed a brand in my mind ... the ultimate Purple Goldfish.

> Last summer I was visiting Palm Beach with my son. Just looking to get a little R&R. Some friends who live nearby invited us out for dinner one night, which was great, but I hadn't really packed anything appropriate for my fourteen-year-old son to wear.

> So, we went shopping in town, and of course he didn't find anything that he liked ... I figured that I would just make do, and we went back to the pool.

> While we were sitting there, he remembered a Lacoste shirt that he thought would be perfect. I was thrilled because he rarely cares how he looks, and we were going to be visiting friends.

> We didn't have a car so we needed to take the hotel shuttle downtown, but I was afraid that we would get there too late. So, I called the store only to find out that they were in fact closing for the day.

> I guess the person on the other end of the phone could hear the disappointment in my voice, and she asked

me what was wrong. Half way through my explanation, she interrupted me to ask me where we were
staying. She offered to bring the shirt to us!

So, I told her the size and color, which they had in
stock, and in fact thirty minutes later she personally
pulled up to the hotel to hand deliver the shirt.

That was a wow. Totally made my night and completely changed my perceptions of the brand. I am
now a loyal consumer time and time again, especially
for gift giving occasions. Maybe because every time I
think of the brand, I smile!

Clearly, the brand knows the importance of customer service in the total experience and has made sure
that they deliver on it at the store level. A true Purple
Goldfish!

VIP SERVICE FOR EVERYONE

Brian Millman shared this example with us from Toronto's Porter
Airlines:

> I wanted to send through a Purple Goldfish to help in
> your quest for 1,001. I'm not sure if you have heard
> of Porter Airlines, but it is a short-haul airline that
> flies out of Toronto's City Centre Airport (very cute
> and small airport) and focuses on business travelers.
> It started primarily operating in Canada with one US
> route to Newark but has expanded to fly to Boston,
> Chicago, and Myrtle Beach.
>
> With most airlines, you expect to sit in the typical
> terminal with old rows of seats. At Porter's hub, they

offer a VIP lounge for everyone. The terminal area is set up similar to that of any VIP lounge: a kitchen stocked with FREE soda and water, two cappuccino machines, and free snacks (cookies & chips). Porter also offers FREE Wi-Fi with a power port under every seat as well as 14 computers for those without a laptop.

THIS PURPLE GOLDFISH IS EASY TO WRITE UP

This is a simple, but handy, example from Peter Hurley:

> "Had lunch today at Salute in New York City. Nice up-scale restaurant that caters to a business crowd. Once seated at the table, I noticed a Purple Goldfish. Each table came with a tiny notepad similar to those you would get at a conference or hotel. It was for notes if needed during lunch. The small pad was branded with Salute's marks and contact info. A nice little keepsake compliments of the restaurant."

Purple Goldfish Takeaway: Embrace the purpose of your clientele. If they are dining to conduct business, figure out ways like a little notepad to grease the wheels of commerce.

WHAT'S YOUR THERMOMETER?

Ron Kaufman at Up Your Service shares this simple, yet spirited example:

> A waiter at La Pirogue Resort in Mauritius comes to work each day with a thermometer in his pocket. On the way to the restaurant he takes the temperature of the ocean water and the swimming pool. As he pours coffee and clears plates during breakfast, he

joyfully tells guests exactly how warm and enjoyable their swimming will be that day. What a great way to improve customer satisfaction![70]

TORY BURCH CLIENT BOOK

Personalization is about connecting the dots. Bridging the gap between online history and offline behavior is one way to do that. Retailer Tory Burch has developed a system for customers and employees that marries both. We featured Tory Burch in *Blue Goldfish* highlighting the experience of Doug Logue. We won't share the full story here, but we will share some highlights. At Tory Burch, in-store team members will:

- offer guests not shopping a beverage and an iPad for entertainment.

- remember sizes and styles based upon your shopping history and notes.

- follow up with customers proactively.

To pull this off seamlessly, they use a system called Client Book. The tablet-based system aggregates their data to provide detailed customer profiles that include personal preferences, online activity, and previous order history. Store associates can find sizes, check availability, view recommended items, and add products to a shopping cart. Associates can communicate with customers via e-mail on their tablet. This feature allows associates to thank clients for stopping by, notify customers about sales, recommend products, and schedule appointments.[71]

---

70. http://www.upyourservice.com/
71. http://www.agilone.com/pdf/store-of-the-future.pdf

According to Matt Marcotte, Head of Global Direct to Consumer for Tory Burch, "Client Book enables customers to keep track of previous orders, wish lists and other information from online accounts. A shopper might put something into her wish list late at night, for instance, and a store associate keeping track could have that item ready on the shopper's next store visit or prepare recommendations for other products."[72]

Adding extra service doesn't have to be high-tech. It's often the human touch that matters most.

72. https://www.internetretailer.com/2013/10/01/fashion-retailer-tory-burch-grows-social-media

CHAPTER 14

MANAGING THE WAIT

"The secret to success is to treat all customers as if your world revolves around them."

– Unknown

#7 – WAITING

We spend 10 percent of our lives waiting or so Stan claims he once read on the Internet. The seventh of the ten types of Purple Goldfish focuses on **Waiting**. Waiting is inevitable for your customers, especially if you have a successful business. How you handle those moments and the little extras you offer can make a big difference.

Fundamentally, the Purple Goldfish of Waiting can be addressed in two ways. You can work to reduce the wait time and you can make the wait feel shorter. We support both approaches.

SPA SERVICES INCLUDED

Take Lexus for example. Car services take time, so the best option is to make waiting more bearable. Lexus gives its dealerships carte blanche to create experiences that customers actually look forward to. Lexus gets it and utilizes the "little extras" as a key differentiator in the car ownership experience. Carolyn Ray shared Lexus of North Miami with us:

> At Lexus of North Miami, people who come in for service are entitled to a complimentary spa service at their in-house spa. Services include manicures, pedicures, haircuts, waxing or chair massage. There is a full-service cafe, kids' playroom, fitness center and pool room for waiting customers. Makes coming in for service a total pleasure![73]

We can't help but wonder whether customers come in for the spa or for the auto service! We may never know, but this example is the gold standard of waiting. You've succeeded at making the wait

---

73. http://www.lexusofnorthmiami.com/Websitesurvey

bearable when your customers might want to stay longer than they must because they're enjoying the experience.

BE OUR GUEST

We know you can just hear the lyrics from Disney's Beauty and the Beast:

> *Be our guest, Be our guest, Put our service to the test ...*

It's no secret that Disney understands waiting. Karl Sakas shared with us insight about the wait times at Disney. As you enter a ride's line, the current wait time is posted outside. As you wait, you pass signs that indicate the wait from your current position in line. Here's the thing, though—they're lies. Disney understands that failing to meet expectations is not an option, so they set expectations with a buffer. Let's say the sign says the wait time is 20 minutes, but you breeze through in 16. You're delighted. Let's say the sign said 15 and the actual result is 16. You get the idea. Setting expectations you know you can exceed is a hallmark of managing the wait.

It's more than just signs. In *Blue Goldfish*, we explored some of the technology Disney uses to manage waiting.

In 2008, Disney set off on its Next Generation Experience project with the intent to remove all friction from the Walt Disney World experience. The problem, on the whole, was that families spent more time planning and coordinating their trip and less time enjoying it. Less time making memories means less mindshare for Disney and a lesser chance of a return visitor.

Wired published a lengthy overview[74] of the project in its March 2015 edition and while we can't go into every detail here, the result of the project was Disney's Magic Band. The futuristic wristband, a quintessential example of form and function, allows short- and long-range sensors around the park to identify you. The result? Magic.

With just this identifier, Disney has eliminated a handful of other items to carry and handle. Park tickets? Ready on the Magic Band. Photo Passes? Tagged to your account automatically. Room keys? Replaced by the band. Fast Passes? Schedule them online and check in with your Magic Band. Cash? Just swipe your Magic Band to bill a credit card on file.

With everything coordinated and synchronized with your Disney account and its smartphone app, you're able to experience the park in a new way. Planning Fast Passes in advance allows you to schedule your must-do attractions and allows spontaneity to guide the rest of your trip.

Beyond the surface, Disney can use the bands and sensors to create magical experiences. The signature restaurant Be Our Guest allows you to order in advance and sit down at any table. Magically your food is delivered without your server even asking your name. It's all powered by the Magic Band and a series of sensors.

The Magic Band is truly a platform project with many future implications from enabling characters to know your name without asking or detecting a long wait and rewarding you with another FastPass or a free ice cream coupon. The possibilities are simply endless.

Your lesson here is one of planning and preparation. Creating magic requires an invisible effort of planning and design. When Disney

74. http://www.wired.com/2015/03/disney-magicband/

set out on this project, they weren't responding to problems one-by-one, rather they set out to build a system that removed friction from the Disney experience. This advance planning to eliminate issues and friction for customers is what we call readiness.

We've said countless times before that expectations are increasing, and you need to get (and stay) ahead of the curve. It's exactly what Disney has done, and you have the opportunity to do so as well.

SAFELITE SETS EXPECTATIONS

One prominent example is Safelite's confirmation emails. When you receive a confirmation email from Safelite, it includes a photo of the technician who will be delivering your service. Have you ever scheduled an appointment with a furnace repair or lawn service provider, and then thought, "Wait, do I even know or trust this person being sent to my home?" If so, you're not alone.

To set the customer's mind at ease about the mobile technician coming to fix their car, Safelite developed the Technician Profile Email containing the name, brief bio, credentials, and photograph of the technician who will perform the service. The email, which is sent the night before or the morning of the service, also provides the estimated time of service and location as a confirmation.

According to Safelite, the program has been extremely well received. In fact, 85 percent of customers said they felt more comfortable with the technician coming to their home once they receive the email.[75]

Customers with the Safelite app can even track the estimated arrival of their technician in real-time. We've all waited at home all

---

75. http://legacy.pitchengine.com/safeliteautoglass/safelites-technician-profile-email

day for a technician who was late or never showed up at all. Not with Safelite.

CHECK IN ONLINE WITH SPORT CLIPS

Sport Clips uses its website and mobile apps to manage the waiting process. In real-time customers can see the wait time at all nearby locations. You can check in to hold your place in line. The website will suggest what time you want to actually show up in the store so you only wait a few minutes before being seen. As a bonus, all locations share the same notes about your preferred cut, so you can go to any location with the assurance that they know you.

UGH ... FLIGHT DELAYS

JetBlue flies into the book from Sharon Trainor-Smith. Sharon shared her delayed flight experience with the airline:

> When flights are delayed, [JetBlue] often shows up at the gate with tables full of free water and snacks and then sets up a trivia game for everyone with good prizes such as free flight tickets, gift certificates, etc. The stranded passengers LOVED these bonuses and there was a lot of positive buzz. Plus, by giving out flight tickets, we were incentivized to come back to JetBlue. It turned a bad situation into a really positive group and brand bonding opportunity.

When faced with lemons, make lemonade right away. You can make the best out of a bad situation by being proactive. It's not about the water, snacks, or trivia. It's about what those things represent, which is that you care about your customers. Kudos to JetBlue for bringing a little humanity back to air travel.

SMART MOVES THAT MAKE WAITING LESS PAINFUL

Here's a simple example from the Great Wolf Lodge as reported by *Connecticut Magazine*[76]

> "At peak check in times the lodge has a face painter, juggler and balloon sculptor wandering to entertain guests."

PEANUTS BECOME A TASTY DIVERSION TO WAITING

We talked about them earlier in the book, but it bears repeating. Five Guys Burgers and Fries is one of our favorite Waiting examples. There is a huge box of peanuts when you walk in. In the early days, Five Guys experienced long lines that forced Jerry Murrell and his sons to distribute free, unshelled peanuts to placate waiting customers. The peanuts have become a Five Guys trademark.

BEVERAGES WHILE YOU WAIT

J.Crew flows into the Purple Goldfish Project courtesy of a submission by Jim Joseph, author of *The Experience Effect*

> J.Crew. I'm a huge fan, have been for a while. Brand experience is exceptional, always consistent whether you are at the store, online, or browsing the catalog. Distinct to each of those venues, but always J.Crew.
>
> The shopping experience in store is particularly good. The sales staff all wear the clothing, so you can actually see how things will look. I've had many of them show me how to tie a tie the "just so cool way" they

---

76. http://www.customerthink.com/blog/great_wolf_lodge_takes_a_proactive_approach_to_service

_around_peak_times

are wearing them, or how to roll the cuffs up on a pair of jeans, or how to partner a pair of shoes with new khakis. This is in store, but they also offer a personal shopping service online as well.

I was at one of the Manhattan stores yesterday, and as you can imagine for a Saturday afternoon in December it was packed. Didn't matter though, the service was impeccable. When I walked in the door, I was greeted by a salesperson. I immediately told her that I was looking for a purple jacket for my daughter ... she immediately took me to the back of the store to see three options. I went upstairs to the men's department where the service was just as good, despite the crowds.

With merchandise in hand, I proceeded to the registers where there was a huge long line. Here's the kicker ... more sales people were working the line with buckets of small bottles of water for the people who were waiting. They also helped [customers] select more items while [they] were in line.

Pacific Cafe, a seafood restaurant in San Francisco, takes this idea to the next level and offers free glasses of wine while you wait for a table. They don't accept reservations and it's a popular spot, so the beverage is a nice gesture to extend to patrons as they wait to be seated.

Waiting is inevitable for successful businesses. The most successful ones understand that waiting is part of the experience and do more to reduce and manage the wait. When done well, your customers may even enjoy the wait.

CHAPTER 15

REMOVING FRICTION

"We see our customers as invited guests to a party, and we are the hosts. It's our job every day to make every important aspect of the customer experience a little bit better."

- Jeff Bezos

#8 - CONVENIENCE

Convenience is measured by your customers. It's more than just having the right location or the right speed of service. Rather it's about fitting seamlessly into their lives.

TD Bank gets this fact, perhaps more than any other bank. James Mayer recommended TD Bank via a post from Jim Taggart at the blog *Changing Winds.* Here is an excerpt:

> As [CEO Ed] Clark expressed in an interview with the *Financial Post Magazine*:
>
> The great thing about our model is if I put a branch on a corner in New York City, I know five years later I will have more than 25% of the local business, because at some time in that five years someone will come by at 4:02 pm. Their branch will be closed, they'll look across at our store, this beautiful store, there will be someone giving dog biscuits to somebody's dog, they'll walk in and there's a greeter that's unbelievably friendly, and they'll say, 'So why am I banking at the guy across the street?'
>
> On Sundays we send our bankers out to all the small businesses and say, "You're open, we're open, and you bank with the bank that's closed. It's a very simple concept: Just be open longer and give better service." Clark also noted, for example, that their branch at 2 Wall Street, which opened five years ago, now has $1 billion in deposits.[77]

---

77. http://changingwinds.wordpress.com/2011/02/10/how-to-blow-away-the-competition-through- leadership-why-td-bank-kicks-butt/

Jim makes his point as well as we could. Customers are more likely to avoid pain than to seek out pleasure. Being the most convenient option will win in the long run.

ICE, ICE BABY

Here's a simple yet an effective and noteworthy little extra. Whole Foods enters the Purple Goldfish Project from Claire Gallo:

> "I live in West Hartford, CT. When you shop at Whole Foods and buy fish, meat or poultry … the folks at Whole Foods will offer to give you ice for free. Very nice touch, especially if you have other errands or plan to shop around town."

FIND THE STUFFED ANIMAL

Trader Joe's features Purple Goldfish throughout its in-store experience. Originally submitted to the Project by Amy DeRobertis, here's what she had to say:

> "There's a fun theme going on here—from Giuseppe Joe's to Trader Jose's, the notion of no middle man is seen on its product labels as well as in the mentality of its Hawaiian shirt wearing associates. And the on-going bevy of free samples at its dedicated sampling stations keeps you interested in the constantly evolving choices and happy rather than devastated when your favorite entree goes missing. There's bound to be something just as great coming down the pike."

Jody Padar added:

"There's a stuffed whale that hides at Trader Joe's. If you find him, your child gets a treat out of a treasure box. Then you get to re-hide [the whale]. My kids love to go to Trader Joe's to find the stuffed animal. It keeps them entertained while shopping. Hint: He spends a lot of time in the snack food isle."

Jennifer Phelps (yes, that Jennifer Phelps) added another way Trader Joe's seeks to entertain its junior shoppers:

"TJs has kid-sized shopping carts. It was a great way to keep our two boys busy when they were young. They got such a kick out of pushing their own carts."

Providing ways to keep little ones busy makes the experience much more convenient for those who are spending the money.

PURPLE GOLDFISH SWIM IN SCHOOLS

A school of Purple Goldfish in the Project comes courtesy of Dan Oltersdorf at Campus Advantage. From his blog post, here is Dan's contribution:

Thanks to Barry Moltz, I just read the eBook: *In Search of Your Purple Goldfish* by Stan Phelps. It is brief and it is worth the read. Unlike my *Puking Baby Policy*, the concept of a Purple Goldfish is something that CAN be proceduralized. In fact, that is a key ingredient. A Purple Goldfish is something every customer gets ...

I won't try to give you the entire concept, but in essence, the "Purple Goldfish" is something above and beyond that you consistently give to your customer that sets you apart.

Think of Southwest (your bags fly free), the warm cookies you get every time you check into a Double-Tree Hotel, or for those of you who have ordered from Zappos, their VIP upgrade with free overnight shipping after your second order.

Phelps contends there is no such thing as "meeting expectations" in customer service anymore. We either fail to meet expectations, or we exceed them. Meeting them is a thing of the past and it is NOT ENOUGH.

Read the eBook and think about what your Purple Goldfish are. Here are some ideas from some Campus Advantage properties to get you started:

- Move-ins – Having cold water and snacks in the apartments for people as they are moving in. Having a dedicated staff member during the move-ins whose job is simply to hand out ice pops on a hot day.

- Door to door package delivery – Instead of making residents come to the front desk, we deliver packages to them at their room or apartment

- Milk & cookie carts during finals week.

- Every team member, from CA to porter to GM, provides a friendly greeting 100% of the time to any person we encounter on a property, [whether] prospect or resident.

- Concierge booklet at the front desk with everything from pizza delivery numbers to who to call if you are struggling in your physics class.[78]

HERE'S THE RUB: INVEST IN YOUR CUSTOMERS AND WATCH YOUR BUSINESS GROW

Jake Hillman shared with us how his wife, Sabina, owner of Body Evolution Massage and Wellness Center goes above and beyond for her customers:

> As a massage therapist, her basic job is to help people relax and feel better. What most people do not expect is her knack for the unexpected: coming in on Sundays to accommodate a client's schedule; sending home remedies to support healing, often at her expense; calling the next day to follow-up and find out how someone is feeling. Her clientele has grown not from common marketing, but from uncommon service, care and connection.

SPLITTING SIZES, NOT HAIRS

Nordstrom only has one rule: "Use good judgment in all situations." And it has only one goal: "To provide outstanding customer service."

Ron Kaufman at Up Your Service wrote about a Nordstrom experience that does just that:

> A sales clerk at Nordstrom in the United States sold my friend a new pair of shoes. Measuring his feet, the clerk discovered my friend's right foot was size 9.5 and the left foot was a smaller 9.0. The clerk gave my

---

friend the shoes he needed to achieve a perfect fit: one 9.5 and the other 9.0. I have no idea what the clerk did with the remaining mismatched shoes, but my friend's loyalty to Nordstrom has been secured. Talk about going above and beyond to improve customer satisfaction!

Stan also experienced this signature extra. In his words:

> Back in 1996, I bought a pair of Dr. Martens at Nordstrom in Portland, Oregon. I distinctly remember the experience, as it was the first time I spent over $100 of my own money on a pair of shoes. Doc's doesn't make half sizes and I couldn't get the right fit between a size 11 and a size 12. My feet are about a 1/2 size apart. The salesperson offered to split the pairs. One word: Sold.

Purple Goldfish Takeaway: Do the unexpected little extra to satisfy your customers. Splitting sizes speaks volumes about Nordstrom's beginnings as a shoe store and its commitment to the customer experience.

Convenience also matters for those who are used to a less-than-convenient experience. As Stan has often experienced with shoes, an odd fit makes it hard to find the right pair. How you handle allergies, disabilities, and other special circumstances speaks to your convenience factor for these customers.

GOING ABOVE AND BEYOND FOR THOSE WITH SPECIAL DIETARY ISSUES

Hank Davis wrote about his experience at The Rainforest Cafe:

> Faye and I are both pretty big fans of having others do the cooking for us. We eat out a lot and we also order

in quite a bit. We experience food service customer service on a very personal level. Unfortunately for Faye, her food allergies make dining out a sometimes terrible experience. She cannot have anything dairy and she cannot even come close to anything from the onion family. She cannot even have something that has touched a grill that has had an onion on it. This makes things really tough.

Recently, however, the team at The Rainforest Cafe made it not so tough for her. In fact, they went above and beyond to the point Faye could not wait to get home from her lunch date with a friend to share the great story with me. Here are the five things that happened that absolutely blew her away and made her day at The Rainforest Cafe.

- At The Rainforest Cafe, Faye did not have to volunteer her allergies to the server because the server started off with a great question: "Does anybody have any food allergies we should know about?" She did this with a smile and genuine concern for her guests. Typically, Faye has to initiate an awkward and sometimes uncomfortable conversation about her allergies but not at The Rainforest Cafe.

- At The Rainforest Cafe, her server actually pointed out, with great care and concern, some specific meal options that might match up with her allergies. She made some really good suggestions which, in our experience, is rare.

- At The Rainforest Cafe, the server brought out a separate menu that covered many of the allergy concerns that many of their guests have. This was great and made Faye feel pretty special.

- At The Rainforest Cafe, the head chef came out of the kitchen to say hello, introduce himself, and see if he could help in any way. He guided Faye through their lunch options, made several specific suggestions and then hand-delivered her meal to her after it was prepared. After the meal, he came back to check to see how she liked it.

- At The Rainforest Cafe, the team took it as a challenge to delight and please my better half and that makes me a Raving Fan (shout out to Ken Blanchard) of The Rainforest Cafe. They loved what they were doing, and it made us love their company.

The bottom line is this: I am talking positively about The Rainforest Cafe, I am planning on going to The Rainforest Cafe again, and I am very thankful to The Rainforest Cafe for making Faye's Day. When she is happy, I am happy, and she was definitely happy. [79]

Concerns like food allergies are no small matter to your customer. Go above and beyond to proactively address concerns and demonstrate you care.

---

79. http://saltandpeppergroup.com/blog/2010/12/5-reasons-the-rainforest-cafe-saved-the-day/

ALLERGY FRIENDLY BECOMES A DIFFERENTIATOR

Sarah Gore of STANCE shared an article in *The New York Times* on Hypoallergenic Hotel Rooms at the Hyatt and Fairmont chains. Here is an excerpt from the article by Tara Mohn:

> Even die-hard road warriors need a comfortable place to recharge after a long day. But for business travelers with allergies, asthma and other sensitivities, hotel rooms can be rife with dust mites, mold, animal dander and other allergens that set off sneezing, itchy eyes, headaches and sleepless nights.
>
> Individual hotels have long accommodated guests by cleaning rooms with special products and processes and washing linens in hot water with no or fragrance-free detergent. They have also offered mattress and pillow protectors, rugless rooms and windows that open.
>
> But now two hotel chains, Hyatt Hotels and Resorts and Fairmont Hotels and Resorts, are taking the service even further by designating permanent allergy-friendly rooms with things like medical-grade air purifiers and chemical- and fragrance-free bath products.
>
> Thirty-eight percent of hotels offer some kind of allergy-friendly service in guest rooms, a 14 percent increase in the last two years, according to the 2010 Lodging Survey Prepared for the American Hotel and Lodging Association by STR, a hotel research company.
>
> Hyatt recently announced plans to create hypoallergenic rooms in all of its full-service hotels in North America. The rooms, which will soon total about

2,000 in 125 properties, cost $20 to $30 extra a night and are intended to eliminate up to 98 percent of allergens and irritants. A medical-grade purifier continuously circulates air, Hyatt said.

"This was a market really underserved," said Tom Smith, vice president of rooms for Hyatt.

The number of allergy sufferers is believed to have gone up substantially since the late '70s, said Dr. Darryl Zeldin, senior investigator and acting clinical director of the National Institute of Environmental Health Sciences. Roughly half of Americans are sensitive to at least one common allergen. Different testing methods may account for some of the increase, but better hygiene resulting in less exposure to bacteria is also thought to play a role, Dr. Zeldin said.

Brian Brault, chief executive of Pure Solutions, the company that installs and maintains Hyatt's hypoallergenic rooms, said more than 200 hotels nationwide, including properties at several major brands, had Pure Solutions rooms, but Hyatt was the first to offer them across its brands. Some hotel conference centers also use the technology, he said.

Lisa Abbott, a marketing consultant for nonprofit groups in Oakland, Calif., who suffers from multiple chemical sensitivities, has learned the benefits firsthand of good air quality in a hotel room.

At home, she rarely takes the morning rush hour train, to avoid "breathing in a soup of fumes and fragrances" from deodorant, hair products and freshly laundered clothing. Traveling, she said, has "always been dicey."

But she stayed in one of Hyatt's new rooms on a recent trip to Chicago. "The air is purer," she said. "I slept great. I felt energized both days of conferences. It has just completely opened up my travel options."

Those customers who need a little extra attention often do not receive it. Differentiate yourself by offering that little extra. They'll reward you with loyalty and a willingness to pay more.

CHAPTER 16

HANDLING MISTAKES

*"Customers don't expect you to be perfect. They do
expect you to fix things when they go wrong."*

- Donald Porter

#9 – HANDLING MISTAKES

During one of the first holidays at Stew Leonard's, Stew had a run-in with a customer. The customer had brought back some eggnog and claimed it was spoiled. Stew knew the eggnog was recently made and became incredulous about the possibility. He became defensive and the customer became indignant. The eggnog had cost a little less than a dollar. Without apology, Stew eventually reached into his pocket and curtly handed over a dollar. The customer took the money, stormed off, and vowed never to come to the store again. That night Stew recounted the story to his wife, Marianne, expecting a sympathetic ear. Instead Marianne blasted him. She accused him of essentially calling a customer a liar. Stew realized he made a mistake. The next day, on the way to work, he made a stop at the local stone shop and purchased a 6,000-pound piece of granite. Soon after, the stone was placed at the front entrance to the store. Etched into the granite were two rules:

> Rule 1: The customer is always right!

> Rule 2: If the customer is ever wrong, reread Rule #1.

Many people argue that the customer isn't always right. That may be so, but the idea of erring on the side of the customer will never go out of style. In the words of Walmart founder, Sam Walton, "There is only one boss and that's the customer. And he can fire everyone from the Chairman on down, simply by spending his money somewhere else."

A small percentage of dissatisfied customers actually complain. Imagine the ones who do not. Even when you do not agree with the customer, realize there may be several other customers with the exact same issue. View these customers and their complaints as an opportunity to improve your customer experience.

NOBODY IS PERFECT, NOT EVEN A PERFECT STRANGER

This type of Purple Goldfish will seem like an odd addition to the list. In business we are generally conditioned to never admit failure. Let's face it. We all make mistakes. How we deal with them is the real question. It's important to not only correct the problem but to go above and beyond to make things right.

The idea of proactively admitting to mistakes is totally unexpected. Admit your wrongdoing, ask the customer what they'd like as amends, and then always exceed their request. This is brilliant on so many levels. First, it is Dale Carnegie-esque—admit when you're wrong and do it emphatically. It takes the steam out of a complaint. Second, it involves the customer as part of the solution. Let them be judge and jury. This speaks volumes about your willingness to make things right. Last, exceed the proposed solution. Within reason, take the solution and notch it up one or two levels. This gets back to the idea of being totally unexpected.

WHEN YOU ARE WRONG...

This Nurse Next Door practice comes from the book *"Customer Love"*:

> "Humble Pie. When this Canadian home health care service provider stumbles... they deliver a fresh baked apple pie and a note apologizing for poor customer service. Each year they spend about $1,500 on pies, but they estimate it saves about $100,000 in business going elsewhere. That sounds like pretty strong ROI

as over 70% of customers that take their business else-where do so because of poor customer service."[80]

Purple Goldfish Takeaway: When you're wrong, admit it and make amends quickly. You may save your reputation and create a loyal customer.

A $1.6 MILLION DOLLAR OOPS

We came across a post on *Inside Zappos* that showed just how much Zappos cares about doing the right thing—even when they make an expensive mistake:

> Hey everyone – As many of you may know (and I'm sure a lot of you do not), 6pm.com is our sister site. 6pm.com is where brandaholics go for their guilt free daily fix of the brands they crave. Every day, the site highlights discounts on products ranging up to 70% off. Well, this morning, we made a big mistake in our pricing engine that capped everything on the site at $49.95. The mistake started at midnight and went un-til around 6:00 a.m. When we figured out the mistake was happening, we had to shut down the site for a bit until we got the pricing problem fixed.
>
> While we're sure this was a great deal for customers, it was inadvertent, and we took a big loss (over $1.6 million—ouch) selling so many items so far under cost. However, it was our mistake. We will be honoring all purchases that took place on 6pm.com during our mess up. We apologize to anyone that was confused and/or frustrated during our little hiccup and thank

80. Anderson, Mac. Customer Love: Great Stories About Great Service. Simple Truths, 2008.

you all for being such great customers. We hope you continue to Shop. Save. Smile. at 6pm.com.[81]

Nice job by 6pm.com to admit the mistake and take their medicine. Their willingness to honor those discounted sales is admirable and more importantly a brand defining moment.

We love it when the folks from the C-Suite get down in the trenches. Zappos CEO Tony Hsieh (Shay) is never afraid to address an issue. Here is his update to the original blog post:

> We have a pricing engine that runs and sets prices according to the rules it is given by business owners. Unfortunately, the way to input new rules into the current version of our pricing engine requires near-programmer skills to manipulate, and a few symbols were missed in the coding of a new rule, which resulted in items that were sold exclusively on 6pm.com to have a maximum price of $49.95. (Items that are sold on both 6pm.com and Zappos.com were not affected.)

> We already had planned on improving our internal pricing engine so that it will have a much easier-to-use interface for our business owners. We are also planning on adding additional checks and balances to hopefully prevent this type of thing from happening again.

> To those of you asking if anybody was fired, the answer is no, nobody was fired—this was a learning experience for all of us. Even though our terms and conditions state that we do not need to fulfill orders that are placed due to pricing mistakes, and even though this mistake cost us over $1.6 million, we felt that the

81. http://blogs.zappos.com/blogs/inside-zappos/2010/05/21/6pm-com-pricing-mistake

right thing to do for our customers was to eat the loss and fulfill all the orders that had been placed before we discovered the problem.[82]

MAKING GOOD IN RESPONSE TO THE SNOWPOCALYPSE

From a post by Axel Murillo[83] of Worldwide Business Research:

> Like one of tens of thousands of people traveling this past holiday season, I had booked a JetBlue flight for the day after Christmas to spend quality time with friends and loved ones. However, Mother Nature had other plans. A storm that quickly produced between 12 and 32 inches of snow fell on many areas of the Northeast that eventually caused the cancellation of some 10,000 flights. It certainly earned its title as the "Snowpocalypse," or "Snowmaggeddon" of 2010.
>
> [Editor's Note: Axel's flight was canceled and rescheduled a total of four times. Each of his reschedules was done via Twitter.]
>
> My trip to Austin eventually went off without too many more delays, once again letting me take for granted things like roomier leather seats on coach, and DirecTV for everyone. Since I pretty much only fly JetBlue these days, I tend to forget that other airlines don't offer what I've come to think of as common sense expectations.
>
> A few days after my return to New York, along with all other passengers affected by the "Snowpocalypse," I

82. http://blogs.zappos.com/blogs/inside-zappos/2010/05/21/6pm-com-pricing-mistake

83. http://www.theetailblog.com/customer-experience/one-customers-jetblue-customer-experience/

received an email from Robin Hayes, Chief Commercial Officer for JetBlue Airways that partly read:

"As a token of our appreciation for your patience during last week's snowstorm when we canceled your flight, please accept 10,000 TrueBlue points which you can apply toward future travel to any JetBlue destination."

If I add those to my existing points, I got a free round trip ticket to Austin anytime! I'm more than satisfied; I am fairly star-struck by this rock-star quality treatment! By any conventional means, JetBlue has no responsibility to provide such perks to assuage climate disruptions. But the fact is that they did; that's what I call a phenomenal customer experience.

Purple Goldfish Takeaway: Be proactive when faced with service disruption. Great job by JetBlue to offer the complimentary TrueBlue points.

WHO IS THIS GARY CHARACTER?

Stan went to see Gary Vaynerchuk speak at a MENG (Marketing Executives Networking Group) New Jersey Chapter event in Morristown. Gary was awesome in his typical "no holds barred" fashion. Here's Stan's take on the experience.

I came in with high expectations and he exceeded them.

He shared a recent example from his company, WineLibrary.com. He recounted that a recent order was screwed up via FedEx. It was not Wine Library's fault, but that didn't matter to the customer. A Wine Library staffer drove the shipment down south three hours to the Jersey Shore and hand delivered it to the customer.

The result? That customer immediately reached out to his network over three or four tweets to laud WineLibrary.com and recommend them "hands down" over the competition.

Gary alluded that there might be some other 'branded acts of kindness' coming down the proverbial (New Jersey) turnpike. He talked about the next major snow storm and the possibility of shoveling the driveways of his best customers. Imagine yourself as a customer and Gary shows up at your doorstep, shovel in hand. That's a Purple Goldfish we'd like to see.

SHARPENING THE SCISSORS

Forbes columnist Dean Crutchfield of The Caffeine Partnership offered up this sharp example from Sur La Table:

> Just recently I visited one of Sur La Table's stores in Manhattan with my entire set of Wüsthof knives in search of their door-buster deal of free blade sharpening. I brought in the lot, even the scissors, only to be informed by the assistant (and the small print) that the offer was for only two knives. I was already in the store, so blaming my reading glasses, as one does, I paid for all the knives (bar two) and left feeling duped and disgruntled.
>
> Two days later, after returning home from picking [them] up, I realized there were no scissors. I called, explained and received a very courteous reply that they do not sharpen scissors, and that my set had likely been misplaced so it was best for me to come back in and get a replacement pair free of charge, even though I did not have the receipt. From there, the experience was like floating on air. An absolute delight that led

me to informing the management at the store and
their headquarters that the whole shop experience was
amazing.[84]

Everyone makes mistakes. Despite our best efforts, something will
go wrong. Experience driven brands understand that when you
recover thoroughly, quickly and empathetically, the customer relationship can end up stronger than it was before the mistake.

---

84. http://www.forbes.com/sites/deancrutchfield/2011/12/19/i-experience-therefore-i-shop/

CHAPTER 17

FOLLOWING UP

"Learn to say thank you every time."

- Jill Griffi

#10 - THANK YOU / FOLLOW UP

Following up with your customers, to say "thank you"
or just to check in on their experience has multiple benefits, not the least of which is increased loyalty from those
customers.

A SIMPLE WAY TO "HUG YOUR CUSTOMERS"

Annette Franz helped us learn about Jack Mitchell of The Mitchells Family of Stores. She shared 1to1 Media's post on Mitchells by
Ginger Conlon:

> When was the last time you personally thanked a cus-
> tomer? Sent a handwritten note? Last year Jack Mitch-
> ell wrote 1,793 personal notes to customers of his re-
> tail stores. That's about five notes a day, every day.
>
> Mitchell is CEO of The Mitchells Family of Stores,
> which owns several high-end retail stores, including
> Marsh, Mitchells, and Richards—and is author of *Hug
> Your Customers*. He spoke at The Conference Board
> Customer Experience Leadership Conference about
> connecting with customers on a more personal level.
>
> Every touch-point, every interaction, every detail—
> these are all opportunities to connect with customers
> in way that creates engagement and builds retention.
> "It can be something as simple as a smile," Mitchell
> said. "It's about making a human connection. Connec-
> tions are 'hugs.' And hugs create loyalty."
>
> So do great people, he said. Great product is a given;
> personalized service is where you can really make a
> difference. So the company looks for people who are

honest, positive, competent, nice, and have a passion to listen, learn, and grow. The retailer retains and engages its employees by using them in catalogs and ads, and by providing them with the product and customer information they need to deliver outstanding service. Also, there's no commission, which encourages collaboration. "It [all] helps to increase their commitment to customer service," he said.

A technology backbone is the third leg of the customer experience stool. The company has tracked every purchase by SKU since 1989, and as a result, has a comprehensive database of customers' product and channel preferences—and knows exactly who its top customers are, by spend. The company uses the information to create personalized mailings, send relevant event invitations (e.g., trunk shows), and the like.

This blended high-touch, high-tech approach helps keep customers right where Mitchell wants them—at center of the company's universe—because customer centricity, he said, is profitable. In fact, 72 percent of the retailer's merchandise is sold at full price. "Focus on what's most important," he said. "Customers."[85]

THE POWER OF THE PEN ... AND SOME STICKERS

Gary Vaynerchuk offers up Wufoo in his book, *The Thank You Economy*.[86] The online HTML form developer sends handwritten

85. http://www.1to1media.com/weblog/2011/05/customer_experience_balancing.html
86. http://thankyoueconomybook.com/

thank you notes, sometimes crafted out of construction paper and decorated with stickers.

SAVE THE DATE STICKERS ARE AN ADDED TOUCH

From a subscriber of the Metropolis Performing Arts Center:

> "We have season tickets to our local theater, Metropolis Performing Arts in Arlington Heights, IL. When we receive the tickets in the mail, included are round Metropolis stickers that I can … put on my calendar to remember our theater nights."

A LITTLE THOUGHTFUL PERSONAL TOUCH FROM THE CAPTAIN

Ivan Misner, founder of BNI, shared a blog post from his experience with United:

> Long lines, deteriorating service, flight attendants grabbing a beer and pulling the emergency exit handle to slide out onto the tarmac are part of our vision of airlines these days.
>
> However, I had an experience last week that was truly amazing in this day and age. My wife and I were flying on United from LAX to New Orleans for a business conference. Before we were about to land, Rebecca, the flight attendant, handed me a business card from the Captain. His name is Patrick Fletcher. On the back of Captain Fletcher's card was a handwritten note that said:
>
> *Flight 139, January 19, 2011*

Mr. and Mrs. Misner,

It's great to have you both with us today – Welcome! I hope you have a great visit to New Orleans – we really appreciate your business!

Sincerely, Pat Fletcher

Rebecca (who was a great flight attendant, by the way), told me the Captain wrote these notes to everyone who was a member of their premier level frequent flier club as well as all the first-class passengers. On this day, that was around 12 people. She said he is great to fly with because he really treats the passengers and the crew very well, mentioning that he had brought scones to all of them that morning.

I fly a lot. In the last 20 years, I've probably traveled on over 800 flights all around the world. In that time, I've never received a personal note from the Captain.

Entrepreneurs and major corporations alike can learn from this story. Personal service that goes above and beyond the call of duty can generate great word of mouth.

Captain Fletcher—my hat's off to you. Well done. I think this is a great example of how one person in a really large company can make a difference in a customer's attitude. Your note was creative and appreciated. I hope to be flying with you again.[87]

---

87. http://businessnetworking.com/the-friendly-skies-are-back/

THE FOLLOW UP CALL IS A LITTLE THING THAT MAKES A BIG DIFFERENCE

From Barry Dalton of Customer Service Stories. Barry referenced a post from Kristina Evey. Here is an excerpt from Kristina:

> I love being a mom more than anything else in the whole world, even chocolate. But, one of the things I dread as a mom is getting that phone call from school informing me that one of my children has "Pinkeye." So, last Tuesday, I picked up my daughter from school and headed to the doctor's office for the diagnosis that I already knew was coming and then to the drug store to pick up the prescription drops.
>
> Now, putting drops into the eyes of a six-year-old is no easy feat. Especially when that six-year-old has decided that she is a drama queen and is going to milk the situation for all it is worth. When I picked up the drops, the pharmacist at Rite Aid suggested some methods for administering the drops that might make it easier and less stressful. Nonetheless, the suggested methods were just as torturous as me literally sitting on my daughter and squirting the drops in her eyes.
>
> However, after two days of drops every four hours, my daughter and I came to a point where we did try the pharmacist's suggestion and were able to administer the drops with no drama at all. So, this is a pretty mundane situation. Nothing really noteworthy.
>
> Until ... we get the call from the pharmacist two days later asking how my daughter's eye infection is doing and if we had any problems administering the eye drops. No, this wasn't a call from the doctor's office. It

was the pharmacist from Rite Aid delivering excellent customer service. She was taking the time and interest to call and see how the treatment was working, if we had encountered any problems, and if we had any questions she could answer. She was connecting with me, the customer. The business transaction, for all practical purposes, was complete. She was following up to nurture the relationship. That's effectively managing the customer experience. Now, they may have designed this into the process at Rite Aid. But that's the point—they design a positive customer experience into their plans.

This really might not seem like a big deal until you think about how often this doesn't happen. How many times do you receive a follow up phone call from the provider of the product or service you purchased from to see if there was anything they could help you with? I'll bet it's less often than you think.

The noticeable thing is that it wasn't the physician who treated her, or even that office. I paid them much more for the physician's time and diagnosis than I did the drug store for the drops.

Customer satisfaction comes from the extra step that we put onto our delivery of service. I was happy just to leave the pharmacy with the drops I needed and the fact that they were nice and pleasant to me. I'm delighted that they called to follow up. Even though I know I may pay a little more to go to Rite Aid, the fact that I received that follow up call tells me they care about my business.[88]

---

88. http://www.kristinaevey.com/customer-satisfaction/excellent-customer-service-is-the-best- prescription/

Purple Goldfish Takeaway: We've seen the follow-up call cited a few times in the Project. It's a smart move for the following reasons:

1. Demonstrates you care – The transaction isn't over when money is exchanged. It shows the customer that you are concerned about their satisfaction.

2. Low cost – This is something that can be done by the pharmacist or business owner during a lull in the ordinary course of business.

3. Troubleshooting – The vast majority of people will not complain. Following up allows you to correct any service issues and extend the life of your customer relationships.

PLAYING THE RIGHT CARDS

This example submitted by James Sorensen shows how a little thought can go a long way:

> My aunt recently required outpatient surgery at Advocate Lutheran General Hospital in Park Ridge. When my aunt and I arrived, we were greeted by a receptionist with a smile, met with the insurance coordinator who thoroughly explained the insurance coverage, spoke with the nurse that took extra time to make sure my aunt was comfortable and finally the doctor whom she has grown to trust over the years.
>
> After the surgery, when I arrived to pick up my aunt, a volunteer from the hospital was waiting in front with her and graciously helped her into my car. We stopped by a local restaurant for lunch and my aunt showed me her discharge paperwork along with a card that read "I hope your visit today was excellent." I thought to

myself that's a nice gesture, but a big surprise awaited us when my aunt opened the card and found it was hand signed by people she was in contact with that day.

What a great example of how the health-care system is utilizing unique ways of reaching out to their patients by showing compassion and delivering a memorable experience.

KNOW YOUR CUSTOMERS

Marty Desmond left this example within a comment on Kelly Ketelboeter's post, "What is Your Purple Goldfish?"[89]

Gumba's in Sunnyvale, CA: I went for breakfast with friends at one of our favorite places on Saturday. We sat outdoors for the first time since street construction began months ago. As we were served, I watched how much fun the employees were having. I told my friends that it was great seeing the restaurant busy again and that I knew the construction hurt much of the business on that block.

I went back Tuesday evening for a quick dinner. As I was eating, the owner came up, patted me on the back and thanked me for my business Saturday morning. Then, he told me how happy he was to see my friends and inquired about them. He asked if the dad had found another job, knowing that he was laid off months ago.

89. http://theexperiencefactor.com/whats-your-purple-goldfish/795/

We talked for a few moments more, and then he patted me on the back again, thanked me once more and walked off. I watched him walk away and thought about why I enjoyed that restaurant so much. The food is great, but it's the experience that makes it worth going back.

I realize that no fewer than four of his employees approached my friend to tell them how much they had missed his family. The culture of that business includes personal relationships whenever possible. I think that is a missing ingredient in so many businesses today.

This restaurant has endured six months of lagging sales, due to people wanting to stay away during construction. Yet, they were genuinely concerned about the lives of the people who walked through their doors. To me, every question of "how is your friend" is a Purple Goldfish.

BIG ASS FANS FOLLOWS UP

Big Ass Fans makes ... well, pretty big fans. The first fan 16 years ago spanned 20 feet. The company prides itself on being customer focused and having a direct line to its industrial, agricultural, commercial, and residential customers. To bring this to life, Dave Waltz fills a role called the Customer Advocacy Manager.

Since 2011, Dave's role as Customer Advocacy Manager has been centered on making calls to the customers of Big Ass Fans. He and his team truly care about honest feedback. As a result, customers tend to take his calls seriously and open up more than if they were called by a salesperson. Being proactive makes a huge difference. Studies have shown that fewer than 5 percent of customers will actually complain when they've had a bad experience. Dave is able not only to catch mistakes but also improve processes and product by talking to all customers.

In his follow-up calls, Dave asks three simple questions:

1. Did you receive the product?

2. Do you have any questions?

3. Is everything OK?

This customer service strategy of follow-up has helped Big Ass Fans grow. Sales have increased by 600 percent since 2009. In an interview with Adrian Swinscoe, founder, Carey Smith credits a number of business improvements and the expansion into Big Ass Lighting as a result of Dave's direct feedback from customers.[90]

Beyond simple surveys, are you picking up the phone to follow up with your customers to uncover issues and opportunities like Big Ass Fans is doing? Simply saying following up is one of the simplest ways to build repeat business and referrals.

---

90.   https://www.forbes.com/sites/stanphelps/2015/08/16/losing-customers-over-poor-service-lessons-from-td-bank-big-ass-fans-on-overcoming-indifference/

CHAPTER 18

THE INGREDIENTS

"Existence is no more than the precarious attainment of relevance in an intensely mobile flux of past, present, and future."

- Susan Sontag

MAKING LAGNIAPPE IS LIKE
MAKING JAMBALAYA

Have you ever made jambalaya? It's a bunch of different ingredients all thrown in together. The chef takes a look at what's laying around in the kitchen and throws it all into a pot. Let the ingredients stew with some spices thrown in and voila—you have a yourself a jambalaya.

Over the last few chapters, we revealed the ten types of Purple Goldfish. Unlike jambalaya, you might want to follow a recipe to create your own. In the next section we'll provide you with a step-by-step process, but first let's summarize the ingredients you'll need.

Here are the five main ingredients of a Purple Goldfish or if you are an acronym fan (like Stan is), the R.U.L.E.S.:

Relevant – The item or benefit should be of value to the recipient.

Unexpected – The extra benefit or gift should be a surprise. It is something thrown in for good measure.

Limited – If it's a small token or gift, try to select something that's rare, hard to find, or unique to your business.

Expressive – Many times it comes down to the gesture. It becomes more about "how" it is given as opposed to what is given.

Sticky – It should be memorable enough that the person will want to share their experience by telling a friend—or a few hundred.

KEEPING IT RELEVANT

The first rule and probably the most important ingredient for a Purple Goldfish is **Relevancy**. If it's just a throw-in or swag (stuff we all get), it probably is not that relevant. It needs to be something that is valued by your customer. Let's look at three examples:

THE OVERNIGHT TEST DRIVE: BMW

Stan was once driving up to New Haven on I-95 and noticed an interesting billboard from BMW of Bridgeport[91] that read: BMW wants YOU to take an overnight test drive.

IMAGINE THAT—they are willing to give you "the ultimate driving machine" for an extended period. No driving around with the salesperson and no more imagining what a BMW might look like parked in your driveway.

There is a strong reason why they want you take the car. Here is an excerpt from a JD Power survey:[92]

> "When it comes to the test drive, most shoppers expect to be able to test drive the vehicle for an hour or more, with most premium brand shoppers expecting to test vehicles for five hours or more. Most shoppers also expect to be able to take the test drive on their own, without the salesperson accompanying them."

Strong move from BMW of Bridgeport. Even if those who test drive don't buy, they are probably going to talk, tweet, post, or blog about the experience.

---

91. http://www.marketinglagniappe.com/blog/2010/01/14/bmw-drives-into-the-purplegoldfishproject-at-150/
92. http://forums.nasioc.com/forums/showthread.php?t=1348892

BUY ONE PINT OF ICE CREAM TO GO ... AND GET TWO CONES FOR THE ROAD

How about making a cone in the comfort of your home? Here is what Molly Holtman shared about Toy Boat:

> "Toy Boat, a great dessert shop on Clement Street in San Francisco, throws in two complimentary ice cream cones (cake or sugar, your choice) when you purchase a pint of ice cream. It's kind of fun to eat ice cream in a cone at home. Plus, their rocky road and pumpkin ice creams are fantastic."

This is a thoughtful and simple complimentary touch from Toy Boat. Dare we say sweet genius?

SECOND INGREDIENT: UNEXPECTED

Steve Knox of Tremor (a P&G agency) wrote an enlightened post in *Ad Age* titled, "Why Effective Word of Mouth Disrupts Schemas."[93] The premise of the article is how to leverage cognitive disruption to drive word of mouth. By doing something unexpected, you force people to talk about their experience. Knox shared that our brain remains typically in a static state. It relies on developing cognitive schemas to figure out how the world works. It recognizes patterns and adapts behavior accordingly. It basically doesn't want to have to think. For example, in the US, every time you get into the car, you instinctively drive on the right side of the road. Fast forward and you're on a trip to the UK or Australia. The first time you drive on the left side, it throws you for a loop. It's disruptive to your normal driving schema and it forces your brain to think, thereby it elicits discussion (word of mouth).

---

93. http://adage.com/article/cmo-strategy/marketing-effective-word-mouth-disrupts-schemas/141734/

Our favorite example from the article was a new Secret deodorant that P&G was launching. The deodorant utilized a moisture activated ingredient which kicked in when you sweat. The brand understood that this could be positioned against a traditional schema, i.e., the more you work out, the more you sweat, and the worse you smell. The tagline for the brand became, "The More You Move, the Better You Smell." A staggering 51,000 consumers posted comments on P&G's website about the product.[94]

We began thinking how this idea of disruption applies to the concept of Purple Goldfish. The second ingredient in the lagniappe R.U.L.E.S. is the concept of being **Unexpected**. It's that little something that's an unexpected extra at the time of purchase. It's the unexpected surprise and delight that triggers disruption of our schemas.

Let's face it, most companies fail to deliver an exceptional customer experience. It's only when a brand goes above and beyond that we get shocked. And what happens when we receive that unexpected lagniappe act of kindness? We tell our friends, we tweet it, and we post to Facebook about it. Let's look at three examples:

THE POWER OF AN UNEXPECTED DISCOUNT

Stan was once at the Pepperidge Farm Factory store picking up a few things. There was a senior citizen standing in front of him in line buying a few items. Her total bill was $9.96. The clerk informed her that all purchases over ten dollars received a 20 percent discount and asked her if she'd like to pick out something else. She made a beeline to the Milano cookies which essentially were free once the discount was factored in. She left the store with a smile on her face and a bounce in her step.

---

94. http://www.secret.com/secret-clinical-strength.aspx

Those Milano cookies were an unexpected surprise and it's probable that she will recount that story a few times. Turns out the folks at Pepperidge Farm make Purple Goldfish both literally and figuratively.

AN EXTRA ACKNOWLEDGEMENT FOR A HOTEL GUEST

Jack Monson shared this story from a business trip to Minnesota:

> A few years ago, I was traveling to the Twin Cities often and stayed several times at the same Courtyard By Marriott in the suburb of Eden Prairie since it was close to two clients' HQs. By the third trip in a few weeks' time, I had a nice surprise waiting for me. I walked in after a cold and delayed trip from Chicago to see a big sign in the lobby saying "Welcome Jack Monson." The manager informed me that I was their guest of the week (or whatever the title was) and gave me a card for free breakfast in the morning. Not a huge thing, but guess where I continued to stay every time I had to travel to Minneapolis over the next year?

KLM DOES A LITTLE EXTRA FOR THEIR FANS

Barry Dalton shared this story about the Dutch Airline KLM. Here is the backstory on the KLM program:[95]

> KLM gives small personal gifts at Schiphol Airport to customers who have indicated through social media that they fly with KLM. If you use the location based social networking site Foursquare or place a message on Twitter at @klmsurprise, indicating that you will

---

95. http://klm.prezly.com/klm-surprises-customers

fly with KLM that day, it may just happen that the KLMsurprise team finds you and surprises you.

As soon as someone checks in via Foursquare at Schiphol or another airport KLM flies to, KLM tries to contact him or her through the @klmsurprise account on Twitter. The message hints that KLM has a little surprise. Next the KLMsurprise team comes into action to quickly offer a surprising, personalized gift before the customer is on board.

THIRD INGREDIENT: LIMITED

The third of the R.U.L.E.S. is the concept of being **Limited**. What does Limited mean? If it's a small token or extra, it means selecting something unique to your business. Ideally you want it to be signature to your brand. Something rare, different, or just plain hard to find elsewhere. A limited extra helps you differentiate your offerings, while providing insurance against being copied by competitors. Let's look at four examples:

APPLES AND PRINTS

Gene Willis submitted this gem from the West Coast:

> The Fillmore, a famous San Francisco music auditorium, has hosted everyone from The Grateful Dead to Snoop Dogg. At the end of each show they hand out a limited number of music posters … free. Each poster has its own unique artwork, and the date of the show and artist. People collect the posters, and sometimes look forward to getting the poster as much as the show. Generations of posters are framed and make up

the walls. Also, when you enter the Fillmore, there is a bucket of free apples and someone who welcomes you to the Fillmore. No wonder it's one of the most loved places to see a band perform live.

The posters and apples are brilliant. It scores high on the five ingredients/rules of lagniappe, especially limited:

- **Relevant** – Each is designed with the artist in mind.

- **Unexpected** – The posters are handbills that are distinctive in size.

- **Limited** – A limited run creates that "one of a kind" special feel.

- **Expressive** – The posters are handed out as a keepsake as the concert-goers leave.

- **Sticky** – The posters are a collector's item that folks share and talk about.

DONUT HOLES AND MILK DUDS

There are reasons native Chicagoans and tourists alike consider Lou Mitchell's a must visit. From the donut holes and the milk duds while you wait to the double-yolk eggs that make every dish even more sinfully indulgent, Lou's knows how to do breakfast.

Located in the South Loop, the restaurant has been a Chicago institution since 1923, and decades later, they're still dishing out thick French toast, enormous platters of pancakes, fresh-baked pastries, and of course, those famous skillets. The extras are just as delectable. Lou's boasts pure maple syrup, fresh-squeezed orange juice, and slabs of toast served with every omelet.

Be prepared to make some new friends—chances are good you'll be seated next to strangers at one of the lengthy tables. Even if you don't bond with fellow diners, the employees' perpetually friendly smiles—and free Milk Duds for the ladies—guarantee that you'll want to return soon.

THIS EXAMPLE PACKS A CHOP

Doug Pirnie shared his experience of staying at the Four Seasons and receiving a signature Purple Goldfish when checking out. In Doug's words:

> "At the end of my stay at the Four Seasons in Singapore, they gave me my own personal 'chop'—a stamp with my own insignia on it. Chinese tradition is for all documents to be 'stamped' with the owner's/writer's/artist's chop."

The hand stamp (especially for a Westerner) is something rare and unique. The addition of personalization on the stamp by the hotel makes it special. Two thumbs up for the staff at the Four Seasons who leveraged Chinese heritage to give a sticky, compelling gift with the CHOP.

GUATEMALAN WORRY DOLLS

Besito means "little kiss" in Spanish. It's also the name of an authentic Mexican restaurant based in Roslyn, New York. Lilliam Villafane De Giacomo recounted her experience of enjoying the amazing food but paid special attention to two added value items. At the end of the meal the restaurant hands out wrapped churros and little worry dolls.

The following excerpt from a review in *The New York Times* mentions the churros and worry dolls:

> "The best dessert was the churros given gratis to every table. The warm, long spirals of fried dough rolled in cinnamon sugar were delivered in a white paper bag. Along with them, we were given tiny worry dolls to be put under our pillows to take away worries. My only worry was the amount of delicious food I'd just eaten."[96]

Here is another review from slapphappe:

> A fresh dish of chunky guacamole is created at your table side from perfectly ripened fruits in a molcajete, the authentic Mexican basalt lava version of a mortar and pestle. It was near perfect for my tastes. Even at twelve bucks a pop we occasionally have two bowls. Their beef enchilada, huevos rancheros and chicken enchilada in creamy tomatillo sauce are all very good. Service is excellent. At lunch today we were each sent home with a complimentary "worry doll" and wrapped churros to go. Legend has it that Guatemalan children tell one worry to each doll when they go to bed at night then put the dolls under their pillow and in the morning the dolls will have taken their worries away.[97]

FOURTH INGREDIENT: EXPRESSIVE

The fourth of the R.U.L.E.S. is **Expressive**. Expressive speaks to "how you give" as opposed to "what you give." A Purple Goldfish is a beacon. It's a sign that shows you care. That little extra

---

96. http://www.facebook.com/note.php?note_id=92123312218

97. http://www.urbanspoon.com/r/201/1422800/restaurant/Long-Island/Besito-Huntington

touch demonstrates that the customer matters. Let's look at three examples:

OH, STEWARD ... THERE'S A DINOSAUR IN MY ROOM

One of the signature elements of staying in a state room on a Carnival Cruise is the towel animals. Every night guests return to find one of the 40 different types of towel animals. A cruise favorite, the folks at a Carnival create about seven million towel animals a year. That's a lot of folding.

About five years ago, Carnival released a book called *Carnival Towel Creations*.[98] The 88 pages encompass a "how to" manual on towel animal making. Think it's easy? New stewards at Carnival spend 10 hours of formal training to master the art of the fold.

One of the things that I like about the towel animals is how Carnival has leveraged them across their various touch points. The towel animals been the focus of advertising, PR, direct mail, and have even appeared online. These towel animals literally have "legs."

BELT BUCKLES AND A POST-IT NOTE

From a post by Drew McLellan from Drew's Marketing Minute:

> I am ... A frequent traveler. A wee bit impatient. All about efficiency.

> So it shouldn't surprise you that I have my travel routine down to a science. I can pack for any trip in less than 10 minutes.

---

98. http://cruises.about.com/od/cruisenews/a/050209carnival.htm

I own a TSA approved messenger bag so I don't have to take my laptop out when I go through security. I always wear slip on shoes. And I just ordered TSA approved belts so I can scoot through the scanner without having to re-belt.

When the belts from BeepFreeProducts arrived, I was pretty pumped to open the package. This was the final tweak to my travel ensemble. (I know ... I can't help it. Don't judge me!) But when I dug past the packaging, I found more than the belts.

There was also a handwritten Post-it note thanking me for my order and saying that they'd included a couple extra belt buckles so I'd have some variety to choose from.

On a simple Post-it note. Nothing pre-printed, nothing fancy. Just a note from Jim.

It probably cost him 2 minutes to jot the note. But I felt the love. Why?

It was unexpected: This was my first order from the company so I had no real expectations. I hadn't spent a huge amount of money and they don't have a super sexy website, product, etc. So I wasn't expecting the creativity and the personal touch.

It was personal: If it had been a pre-printed card, it probably wouldn't have been as memorable or noteworthy. He addressed the note to me, not "dear customer or sir." Whether it's true or not, I felt like Jim really did want me to have those extra buckles. He really cared that I could mix and match my buckles.

Many people believe that creating a lasting love affair with your customers is going to be incredibly expensive. It doesn't have to be. In fact, you can't buy their love. If you try too hard or it feels like you are throwing money at it, rather than throwing your heart into it, it will backfire. Instead of them feeling your love, they'll feel a little cheap, like you think they can be bought. But let Jim's Post-it note remind us all that it's the heart that counts, not the cost.[99]

IT'S NOT ABOUT THE MONEY

Examples from BMW, Les Schwab Tires, and The Four Seasons... Total Cost = $0

BMW of Darien courtesy of Jack Sarsen:

> When I dropped my car off for service, I had to move 2 car seats to the loaner. Upon my return, a service guy, obviously recognizing the number on the car, walks out to the loaner as soon as I parked and told me to hold tight. Within a minute my car pulled up and two service guys helped me make the car seat switch with my small children in tow. Another walked out and handed me my paperwork and said, "Thank you, have a nice day."

Les Schwab Tires from Cody Goldberg:

> "The service people jog to your car when you pull in to the service center."

Four Seasons Hotel from Stephanie Hadden:

---

99. http://www.drewsmarketingminute.com/2010/11/creating-love-affairs-you-cant-buy-their-love.html

"When you check in, the front desk attendant will walk around to the front of the counter and hand you your key while using your name and anticipating your every need. This customer service costs them nothing extra but makes you feel like a million bucks."

Purple Goldfish Takeaway: You don't have to tap into big dollars to go the extra mile. Being quick, responsive, and alert with your customer service can make all the difference.

FIFTH INGREDIENT: STICKY

STICKING OUT IN A SEA OF SAMENESS?

The fifth of the R.U.L.E.S. is **Sticky**. You want something that sticks. A strong Purple Goldfish promotes word of mouth. Your Purple Goldfish needs to be memorable and talkable.

Two questions to ask yourself: Is it water cooler material? And will your customer tell three people or 3,000?[100] Let's look at four examples:

DROPPING THE STICKY BOMB

Phil Gerbyshak nominated AJ Bombers to the Purple Goldfish Project. In Phil's words:

> One of my favorite Purple Goldfish is AJ Bombers (@ ajbombers) in Milwaukee. Joe [Sorge] and his team consistently provide the Purple Goldfish by offering free peanuts ... shot at you in metal WWII bombers. It's way fun to get those from the bartenders. Making

---

100. http://www.tell3000.com/

AJ Bombers even more fun is the fact he is on Twitter, recognizing customers and anyone who mentions the place; hosts Tweetups at Bombers; has guest bartenders where he donates shots folks can sell ... with all proceeds going to the charity of the guest bartender's choice. Full disclosure: I've been a guest bartender and raised money for my charity. Last but not least is everyone who wants one can get a Sharpie and put their Twitter handle anywhere they want at AJ Bombers, so when friends come in, they can look for your Twitter name and leave you a tweet ... in real life.

Of the five main ingredients or R.U.L.E.S., Bombers scores huge on stickiness. As Phil told us, the bartenders at AJ Bombers literally send bombers attached to rails above the bar to deliver the nuts. Joe Sorge shared an interesting wrinkle:

> "By the way, not only do we offer free p-nuts to our guests while they are at the restaurant, they always get BONUS unexpected nuts with all 'to go' orders. Their reactions are priceless, they love it."

Here is a rundown of the Top 5 Purple Goldfish from AJ Bombers:

1. P-nut Bomber – This is a signature way to deliver peanuts to the respective booths.

2. Oversize Beach Chairs – You feel like a silly little kid while sitting in one of their larger than life beach chairs. (But isn't that the point?)

3. Quad Cow – Take on the quad cow at AJ Bombers if you dare. After you've swallowed the last bite of your four-patty burger, you can sign your name on the sacred cow that adorns the wall.

4. Sharpies – Grab a marker and leave your name or Twitter handle on the wall. You are now part of AJ Bombers.

5. Streamlined menu – Your menu is a narrow piece of paper that details the various burgers. Grab a pencil and start writing — choose well.

A HANDFUL OF GOLDFISH ... PLUS A REAL PURPLE COW

Phil also shared another gem from Milwaukee:

> I was just thinking about one of my favorite Milwaukee Purple Goldfish, Pizza Shuttle. From the original Andy Warhol "Purple Cow" in the dining area, to the fantastic hold messages, to the old Pizza Shuttle trading cards they let people collect of their drivers, to the fact you get free pizza on your birthday, to the in-store photo booth perfect for taking pictures, it's all fun. Couple that with late-night delivery of pizza AND frozen custard AND chicken AND burgers [and the] fun, unique people who work there and you get an amazing place to eat and an experience for everyone. A few other wonderfully inventive things they do: The world's largest pizza, available for dine-in only; An amazing program where they give back HUGE to the community they serve; Delivery to all the colleges, hotels, and universities in the area; Employing nearly 100 people in a town that can desperately use it.

Businesses that tend to get the concept of Purple Goldfish usually have multiple Purple Goldfish. They understand that in order to stand out you need to differentiate by giving those little unexpected extras. Pizza Shuttle is no exception. Here is a summary of their top four:

1. The Purple Cow (hat tip to Seth Godin) – How many pizza places have a framed Andy Warhol on display? Genius interplay of pop culture and a homage to the dairy state of Wisconsin.

2. A Picture Booth – Take your experience home with you with a branded strip of black and white photos. Great memento for a date with your squeeze or a night out with your friends. A picture may be worth a thousand pizzas.

3. The Largest Pie in Wisconsin – Be memorable by offering a $39.95 gut buster pizza. According to an article by Jason McDowell,[101] it looks like they throw in ice cream as an added lagniappe.

4. Unique hold music – Can you imagine wanting to be put on hold? Create some fun messages so people can be entertained while they wait. Smart move when you have a robust delivery business.

PROMOTING WORD OF MOUTH USING SPARE CHANGE

A clean example from a post by Ben Popken at *The Consumerist*:

> As a favor to guests, one hotel washes every coin it receives, just like it's done since 1938. The practice at the St. Francis Hotel in San Francisco is said to have started when hotelier Dan London observed that some coins sullied a woman's white gloves. At the time,

---

101. http://onmilwaukee.com/dining/wineanddine/articles/pizzashuttlepizza.html

coins were used for everything from tips to payphones to taxicabs. Back then washing the coins [was] a full-time job. Now it's only 10 hours a week, but the practice continues, passed down from one generation to the next.

The coins are first passed from the general cashier to the coin washer who dumps them into a silver burnisher. Along with the coins, the burnisher is filled with water, buckshot to knock the dirt off, and a healthy pour of 20 Mule Team Borax soap. After three hours of swishing the coins around, Holsen uses a metal ice scoop to pour the loot into a perforated roast pan that sifts out the buckshot. The wet coins are then spread out on a table beneath heat lamps. This is where once-rusted copper pennies turn into shimmering bronze coins. Quarters look like sparkling silver bits.[102]

Purple Goldfish Takeaway: Do guests of the St. Francis really care that their coins are sparkly? Other than the germophobes, probably not. But this Purple Goldfish ranks extremely high on Sticky.

HOW DO YOU OVERTAKE A LUXURY BRAND WITH THE HERITAGE OF MERCEDES-BENZ?

While preparing to launch an unknown brand with no heritage against established European brands such as BMW and Mercedes, Japanese automaker Lexus set out to build the perfect car and retail experience. Nothing less than a "relentless pursuit of perfection" was the mandate when the brand was launched in 1989. Twenty-three years later the brand is all grown up. It's kicking ass and

---

102. http://consumerist.com/2010/12/hotel-washes-every-coin-they-get-as-courtesy-for-guests.html

taking nameplates. One of the ways that Lexus distinguishes itself is through its customer service and by doing the little talkable extras.

Ray Catena Lexus of Monmouth, New Jersey treats each customer as they would a guest in their own home. It's as simple as making sure the coffee is always fresh, the loaner car is always clean, or just giving a friendly smile and hello when passing a customer in the showroom.

1. FORE!!! When you drop your car off for service at Ray Catena Lexus, bring your golf clubs. You can practice your game at an indoor driving range and golf course simulator adjacent to the plush waiting lounge.

2. Follow-up - Dedicated to making sure your experience was perfect, Ray Catena has one person whose sole job is to call people who have had warranty service to make sure everything went smoothly. According to a *Forbes* article:

   "Customer surveys revealed that 99.2% of people who serviced their cars at the store would recommend it. That meant there were about a dozen less-than-perfect surveys out of 1,400. Those customers got personal letters and phone calls offering apologies."[103]

3. Free Car Wash – A staple of the Lexus service is the free car wash. I was talking with Shelley Grosman, a co-worker who brings her car into Ray Catena for service. We discussed their service and she started gushing about how they are so committed and that everything is always done just right. When Shelley mentioned the car wash, I shared my feeling that the free car wash has become expected, kind of like the baker's dozen. It loses a little bit of its specialness if everyone is doing it. Audi,

---

103. http://www.forbes.com/forbes/2004/0621/068_print.html

BMW, and VW have also been cited in the Project for the car wash. Shelley mentioned that on a recent trip that the wait for her car to be washed was long. Lexus apologized and handed her a voucher for a car wash down the street. Another time Lexus couldn't wash her car because of the constant rain. Instead they filled her gas tank on the house.

The R.U.L.E.S. provide an overview of what you should keep in mind as you create your own Purple Goldfish. Now that we're inspired with examples from the companies featured in Section II, we'll move into Part III that outlines our step-by-step process for creating your own Purple Goldfish.

CREATING YOUR OWN PURPLE GOLDFISH (THE HOW)

CHAPTER 19

THE I.D.E.A. PROCESS

"There is one thing stronger than all the armies in the world, and that is an idea whose time has come."

– Victor Hugo

Since the release of *Purple Goldfish* in 2012, we've trained hundreds of companies and organizations. As you might imagine, it's not enough to help an organization understand what a Purple Goldfish is and why they need them, organizations also need help creating their own Purple Goldfish, so we developed the I.D.E.A. Process.

The I.D.E.A. Process was originally called 3D Design—Discover, Design, and Deploy. Over time we decided that the ideas leaving the design step needed more consideration before deployment, so it evolved into Design, where you generate ideas, and Evaluate, where you pilot those ideas before rolling out. Since we'd then lost our series of words that begin with D, it was time for a new acronym: I.D.E.A.

Of course, we love a good acronym. In fact, the only thing Stan loves more than an acronym is an acronym and a portmanteau all in the same word, but we digress.

Here's the overview of the I.D.E.A. Process:

Inquire – understand what is important to your customers and what gaps and opportunities exist in your current customer journey

Design – generate ideas for Purple Goldfish (we call them Purple Goldfish Fry, or PGF for short) to address the gaps and opportunities in your current customer journey

Evaluate – complete internal analysis and external pilot to determine which PGFs, should be rolled out across the organization

Advance – bring your best PGFs out of the pilot phase and into widespread rollout, measuring the results and creating a feedback loop back to the Inquire phase

In the next four chapters we'll walk you through the steps of the I.D.E.A. Process. If you decide you want to follow the I.D.E.A. Process in your organization, consider picking up the *Purple Goldfish Workbook* on Amazon, which provides exercises to guide you through each stage of the process. We believe it's helpful and we think you will too.

CHAPTER 20

INQUIRE

A subtle thought that is in error may yet give rise to fruitful inquiry that can establish truths of great value.

- Isaac Asimov

I nquire is to ask questions to find direction. During the inquire phase you're going to ask lots of questions of both people and data.

Before you undertake the creation of a Purple Goldfish, you must first understand the big picture, something CX professionals call the customer journey. By understanding your customers' journeys, and that no two are alike, you can discover the gaps and opportunities to create Purple Goldfish. Let's start by learning more about customer journeys, gaps, and opportunities.

CUSTOMER JOURNEYS

As the name implies, a customer journey is everything your customers experience as they interact with your brand before, during, and after purchase. Think for a moment about the last time you used a hotel. Could you list every interaction you had with the hotel before, during, and after your purchase? If you could, your list might look something like this:

- Decide to take a trip

- Research places to stay

- Select an area of town

- Look for hotel options

- Compare hotels

- Select a hotel

- Compare hotel rooms

- Book a hotel room

- Travel to your destination

- Locate your hotel

- Enter the lobby

- Wait for a front desk clerk

- Check in

- Find your room

- Open the door

- Walk inside

- Stay one or more nights

- Check out of your room

- And then travel back home

- Tell others about your experience

This might seem like a long list. We certainly grew tired as we were writing it, but it only scratches the surface of what steps a customer might take in their journey with your company. CX professionals would call each of these steps a touchpoint, and we study touchpoints on what we call a journey map, but before we create journey maps, we need to gather insights about our customers.

CUSTOMER INSIGHTS

There isn't a right way to gather customer insights, but there are plenty of wrong ways. Let's start with the most common one. It sounds something like this: "We've been in business for thirty years.

We know exactly what our customers want." Cue the dramatic music. The biggest trap you can fall into is assuming you know exactly what your customers want. Sure, you likely have a good sense of their needs, but there's always so much more you can learn.

There are entire books on gathering customer insights, so we won't try to recreate that here, but what we will offer are some thoughts on the best sources of customer insight. As you prepare to map your customer's journey, you want to answer the following questions:

- What do our customers care about? Which one do they care about most?

- What do customers expect from similar organizations?

- How well do we meet their expectations today?

- What are common points of failure for us?

As you seek to answer these questions, there are numerous sources of input that may be helpful. Here are a few that we suggest our clients turn to:

- **Customer data** – What data does your organization gather that might provide insights into your customers?

- **Surveys** – Do you conduct any customer or employee surveys, including Net Promoter or Customer Effort scores?

- **External data** – Are external data or reports available about your customer segment?

- **Interviews** – Can you sit down and interview a sample of your customers?

- **Win-Loss Analysis** – Have you conducted an analysis of customers you didn't win or customers you lost?

- **Proxies** – If you don't have direct access to customers, who interacts with them most (e.g. front-line employees) and can you interview them?

- **Observations** – Can you observe customer interactions either in-person or via recordings?

Often CX professionals will document insights about customers in a document called a persona. Customer personas are profiles of prototypical customers, based on data from actual customers. Often these personas will be organized by the type of customer. For instance, a hotel might have different personas for business travelers, leisure travelers, and event planners, to name a few of their key audiences.

In our workshops, we often create proto-personas. These are persona-like documents that allow our participants to get the feel of creating personas but are often based on their personal experiences and not on customer data. Proto-personas can be helpful for training or for creating a first draft of personas but must be validated by data to be useful.

Personas are great at documenting what your customers want, but often do not include how well you perform against their desires. For that exercise, we often create an Attribute Map[104]. An Attribute Map is a graph where you list your customer's needs on one side in rank order and then rate your relative performance on a scale of 0-11. Here's an example:

---

104. Frances Frei and Anne Morriss, *Uncommon Service*

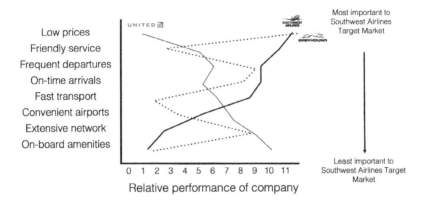

As you can see, the map clearly shows what your customers need and where you fall short. This high-level exercise can help you decide where to focus your CX efforts or can inform the journey mapping process in the next step.

Armed with customer insight, either in its raw form or organized into personas, you now know what your customers want and expect. The Attribute Map and other data about your current performance give you the raw insights that will help you document your customer journey in step two and then identify gaps and opportunities in step three.

INQUIRE PHASE PROGRESS

✓	Step One: Gather Customer Insight
	Step Two: Create Journey Maps
	Step Three: Identify Gaps and Opportunities

JOURNEY MAPS

Journey maps are designed to create a sense of empathy. By looking at all of your customer touchpoints, good, bad, and ugly, all on one document, you can step into the customer's shoes and feel their pain or delight. Of course, the latter is what we're going for.

In our workshops, we encourage participants to create both current state and future state journey maps. The current state documents what is happening today, while the future state is the journey you might aspire to create.

You can choose to create a high-level journey map that covers all steps of the customer's journey but with less detail or you can choose to create a detailed map for a specific segment of the customer journey to help you perfect a critical part of the journey.

Journey maps do not have to be exhaustive, in fact it's easy to get caught up on creating the most exhaustive journey map possible. We believe this takes your focus away from actually solving your customers' challenges or worse causes you to miss the proverbial forest (big picture) for the trees.

In our workshops, we often ask participants to organize their journey maps in rows by the touchpoint's medium, as different touchpoints happen via social media, via the Web, in-person or, in some cases, through a reseller or agent.

There are a number of great resources out there on journey mapping, so we won't seek to reinvent that wheel here, but getting back to our hotel example, here's a list of journey maps you might choose to create and how they could be useful.

- **The booking experience** – a detailed journey map including all of the steps needed to book a room, divided by channel, which includes social media, the hotel website, the call center, travel agents, and travel booking websites. You would use this map to look for gaps and opportunities to streamline and simplify the booking process.

- **The in-room experience** – a detailed map of the things a customer might choose to do from their guestroom and the related touchpoints. This map could include everything from making coffee, using the iron, and ordering room service. You would use this map to make improvements to your facilities, amenities, or customer service.

- **The high-level experience** – a not-so-detailed map of every phase of the customer's journey with your hotel, with external factors included. This might resemble the list earlier in this chapter. Some external factors might include a flight delay or other travel irritation. You would use this map to help team members have greater empathy for the customer and look for opportunities to improve a customer's trip, even if you didn't cause the underlying issue.

There are all sorts of ways to approach journey mapping and there's no right answer, except that you must consider two factors:

1. Does the journey map give you enough detail to understand how you might improve the customer's experience?

2. Is the journey map based on actual insights from your customers, data about your customers, or insights from your front-line employees?

If the answers to those questions are anything other than a confident yes, you likely need to adjust your approach.

INQUIRE PHASE PROGRESS

✓	Step One: Gather Customer Insight
✓	Step Two: Create Journey Maps
	Step Three: Identify Gaps and Opportunities

GAPS AND OPPORTUNITIES

A few times during this chapter we've mentioned gaps and opportunities. Now it's time for us to talk more about those.

A gap in your customer journey is a failure or a breakdown. These are points along the journey where your business processes get in the way of the customer's goal or do not serve customer needs. The result is often customer frustration.

Unexpected cases of customer frustration can occur as well. Journey mapping helps you minimize these cases, but they always will exist, so create an "issue resolution" journey map to plan how you might handle the occasional mis-step or mistake. Chapter 16 goes into more detail about this.

But those one-off mistakes aren't what we mean by gaps. Gaps are systemic breakdowns in your customer experience. For instance, at one of Evan's previous companies, a journey mapping process revealed a common point of customer frustration. As soon as a contract was signed for a new software subscription, the customer's subscription was activated, and they were billed for setup fees and their first month's fee. Sounds reasonable, yes? But what the journey map revealed was a delay—often by as much as several weeks—before the customer was able to begin using the software. The systemic gap was a customer paying for something they were not yet receiving value from. As we learned in Chapter 12, first impressions matter and this company was not making a good one.

It's worth noting that Evan's current company, which is also his own company, has a billing process that avoids this gap. He doesn't bill clients until they've felt value from the relationship. Often times that is after a kick-off meeting or an initial consultation. To be clear, we're not suggesting you take the same approach in your organization as your circumstances may be different. What we do hope is that you now understand the difference between a gap, which is a systemic issue, and a one-off issue. It is worth noting, however, that if the same one-off issue keeps coming up, you might want to investigate the root cause to see if it's actually a systemic issue.

As you review your journey map, think of gaps as valleys or potholes. These are the parts of the customer experience you want to address. Speaking of potholes, let's use a roadway analogy for a moment.

Let's say that your customer journey resembles a road that is flat and straight, and you've pointed out several potholes. Suppose you use all of your budget to fill every pothole, but you still have a road that's flat and straight. While there are no issues riding down your road, there's also not much excitement.

Now envision a curvy mountain road—the kind of road where motorists will travel from afar to experience. There are twists, turns, views, and any number of hazards that create a thrill. Let's say that there are also a fair number of potholes.

Which road would you rather experience? The perfectly maintained but boring pavement or the exciting but imperfect one? We suspect it's the latter.

In the *Power of Moments*, Chip and Dan Heath caution against using all of your resources to address gaps. They advocate for the creation of peak moments. That is investing in experiences that are memorable and stand out.

Gaps are easy to find and easy to spend all of your time chasing. If you do that, however, you'll engage in a never-ending game of Whack-A-Mole and never create an experience that is remarkable. We encourage you to address your largest gaps, but also spend time identifying the opportunities to create a peak moment. Some of the best Purple Goldfish create peak moments for customers.

Identifying opportunities is much more difficult than looking for gaps. Opportunities can exist in a gap. For instance, you could choose to double down on a common gap in your industry not only to solve it but to turn it into a peak experience.

This reminds us of Disney's Be Our Guest restaurant. A common gap in restaurants is wait time. Disney addressed this by creating an order-ahead system so that you spend minimal time waiting for your food at your table. Using their Magic Band system, they've also sought to make this a peak experience where they can deliver your food almost as soon as you are seated (because the RFID in the Magic Band tells them when you arrive and to begin preparing your order). They take the experience to the next level by having servers address you by name without asking your name first. The Magic Band system tells them who's who. And it's especially exciting for kids to experience the "magic" of everyone knowing their name.

For the most part, however, your opportunities won't come from gaps. They will come from ordinary experiences. We ask our workshop participants to review their journey maps for ordinary moments that might resonate with their customers.

For instance, consider The Durham Hotel in Durham, North Carolina. The retro-chic boutique hotel is a haven for today's modern consumer. The property features a gourmet coffee bar and a lavish rooftop patio not to mention well-designed, modern guestrooms. Knowing that their hotel attracts a foodie audience, they decided to transform the in-room coffee experience. A coffee pot is a staple of most US hotel rooms. Most hotels purchase filter packs of Starbucks or another recognized coffee brand and ensure rooms are well-stocked. Some hotels take it to the next level with an in-room Keurig and a selection of K-cups. The Durham, however, takes a different approach. Each guestroom has a door hanger that resembles a breakfast room service menu, except that at The Durham the card lists a choice of beans from Durham-based Counter Culture, one of the top five craft roasters in the country. The card allows you to select your beans and the time of day when you would like for your freshly ground coffee to be delivered. Oh, and did we mention that the coffee service is complimentary? In the morning, by your chosen time, you'll have a sealed packet of your freshly-ground coffee choice waiting for you outside your door. Talk about a "perk."

Before creating this experience, we're certain that The Durham didn't see coffee as a gap. Customers are generally not expecting a gourmet, in-room coffee experience, but it was an opportunity to create a peak moment.

INQUIRE PHASE PROGRESS

✓	Step One: Gather Customer Insight
✓	Step Two: Create Journey Maps
✓	Step Three: Identify Gaps and Opportunities

Now that we've completed the Inquire stage, it's time to start creating Purple Goldfish. Let's move into the Design phase of the I.D.E.A. Process.

CHAPTER 21

DESIGN

"Design is not just what it looks like and feels like.
Design is how it works."

- Steve Jobs

D esign is the most exciting part of the I.D.E.A. Process. It's where you generate ideas, some of which may very well be innovative, to better serve your customers. Ideation is rarely a linear process. Some ideas come from an epiphany and others build on each other.

While ideas come to us when we least expect them, there are ways to organize the ideation process and that's exactly what we recommend during the Design phase. This phase calls for you to brainstorm your Purple Goldfish Fry (PGF) around the gaps and opportunities you identified during the Inquire phase.

The goal during the design phase is to generate as many ideas as possible, whether or not you believe they will be immediately viable. Often the best ideas come from creating a more reasonable or measured version of an idea that's too big, complicated, or expensive to implement.

SET YOUR FOCUS

As we discussed in the previous section, your goal should not be to fill every gap you identified. Instead your goal is to address the gaps that are most damaging to your customer experience. In an ideal world, this will leave budget, time, and other resources to create peak moments for the most promising opportunities.

To this end, your first step in the Design phase is to choose which gaps and opportunities you would like to address. Starting from the list you created, first identify which gaps are the most damaging. Here are some questions you can ask to help you prioritize the list:

After which gaps do we tend to

- lose the most customers?

- see NPS or other measures drop?

- receive the most complaints?

As you ask these questions and rank the gaps accordingly, chances are good that a few will bubble to the top. Those 3-5 top gaps are the ones that should grab your design attention.

We also encourage you to repeat this ranking process for opportunities but using a different set of questions to determine the most promising ones. Here are questions to get started:

Which opportunities

- are directly related to your core product or service?

- are most important to your target customers?

- will serve the majority of your customers or prospects?

- will create competitive separation in the marketplace?

- are unlike anything you've done before?

As you can imagine, ranking opportunities is a bit harder. The process requires intuition and will feel more squishy than ranking gaps. This is exactly why so many companies fall into the trap of only addressing gaps. Our rational brains far prefer the certainty of addressing known gaps to the uncertainty of creating something brand new. Embrace the uncertainty.

At this point add your 3-5 opportunities to your list of 3-5 gaps. These are your areas of focus for the Design process. You might have completed this ranking alone or with a group. If you worked alone, now is the time to get others involved.

DESIGN PHASE PROGRESS

✓	Step One: Set Your Focus
	Step Two: Ask Big Questions
	Step Three: Organize Your Ideas

ASK BIG QUESTIONS

Just before the brainstorming portion of our workshops, we ask participants to complete an exercise. We give each person a blank sheet of paper and ask them to draw a picture of a vase with flowers. Within about 30 seconds, most everyone, regardless of artistic talent, sketches out a container with one or more flowers. We then ask them to draw a second picture. This time, however, we ask them to draw a better way to enjoy flowers in their home. As you might imagine, we receive many different drawings. Often, we go around the room and ask each participant to explain their idea.

We call this a design thinking exercise. Psychologically speaking, it's an example of divergent and convergent thinking. Both terms were coined by psychologist Joy Paul Guilford.

Divergent thinking is a thought process or method used to generate creative ideas by exploring many possible solutions.[105]

Convergent thinking is the opposite of divergent thinking. It generally means the ability to give the "correct" answer to standard questions that do not require significant creativity.[106]

During the exercise, the first prompt—drawing a vase—is a convergent thinking exercise. While some creativity is involved, there is

---

105. https://en.wikipedia.org/wiki/Divergent_thinking
106. https://en.wikipedia.org/wiki/Convergent_thinking

generally one correct answer. The second prompt requires divergent thinking as we're asking participants to come up with a possible solution to the problem and not one correct answer.

You might be wondering what this has to do with designing your Purple Goldfish. Everything, in fact. This exercise exists to awaken the parts of our brains that handle divergent thinking. As we start the brainstorming process, we're not looking for the most correct or logical ideas. Rather we are seeking many possible solutions to address the given gap or opportunity.

Harvard Instructor Anne Manning notes that divergent thinking is useful for coming up with ideas and convergent thinking is good for making decisions about those ideas, but it's difficult to do both at the same time.[107] During the Design phase, you and your team should focus on divergent thinking and avoid the temptation to question or evaluate ideas.

We recommend a group brainstorm for generating ideas. There are whole books on the art and science of brainstorming, so we'll just cover our tips for the process.

1. **Environment** – Create an environment for generating new ideas. You might want to consider hosting the brainstorm at an off-site location or perhaps immediately after touring one of your retail locations, if you have them.

2. **Supplies** –Make sure everyone has what they need to be productive—coffee, water, snacks, office supplies.

3. **People** – Get the right number of people in the room. Brainstorming works best with 5-8 people. Beyond that number, some will mentally check out of the process.

---

107. https://www.youtube.com/watch?v=xjE2RV6IQzo

4. **Cross-pollination** – In our workshops, participants are often grouped with others from their teams in the company. This can work well as can intentionally mixing departments to generate different perspectives. We like and use both methods and encourage you to experiment with what works best for you.

5. **Focus and timing** – We recommend focusing on one gap or opportunity at a time. Perhaps consider setting a timer or a goal for total ideas and once completed, moving on to the next gap or opportunity.

6. **Format** – In our workshops, we often ask for individuals to first come up with ideas and then share them with their brainstorming group. Sometimes we use sticky notes to collect all of the individual ideas.

7. **Yes, and** – Remember, the purpose of the exercise is to generate as many ideas as possible, not to evaluate them. You'll want to set strict rules about not dismissing or contradicting any ideas. A helpful way to do that is to start ideas with "yes, and" while avoiding words like "but" and "however" (and other creative phrases to contradict without using these words).

We called this section "Ask Big Questions" and now that we're set up to brainstorm, we finally get to ask those big questions. We find that it's helpful to ask thought-provoking questions around each gap or opportunity to elicit different ideas to address them. During the brainstorm, your facilitator may choose to ask some of these questions to help elicit ideas.

Here's our go-to list of questions:

- If it were magic, how would it happen?

- If we eliminated x altogether, what could we replace it with?

- What is the confusing part about x?

- How have others solved x?

- If you had a budget of one million dollars, how would you solve this problem? What about a budget of ten dollars?

- If you had a year to solve this problem, how would you do it? What if you had ten minutes?

You will likely develop some of your own questions as well. We like questions that go to the extremes, as you can see with the last two questions focused on budget and timeline. Often times the best ideas come from the pared back version of a much larger, but infeasible idea. Those questions help develop those big ideas.

As you finish the brainstorming process, make sure you've captured all of your ideas. Taking photos of whiteboards, sticky notes, and flipcharts can be helpful. These will be important reference materials as you move into the next step.

DESIGN PHASE PROGRESS

✓	Step One: Set Your Focus
✓	Step Two: Ask Big Questions
	Step Three: Organize Your Ideas

ORGANIZE YOUR IDEAS

Now that you've generated many ideas, some of which are likely extraordinary, you'll want to organize them in a uniform way for internal consumption and evaluation. There's no right way to undertake this process, but we do have a few recommendations.

Start by stating the gap or opportunity you're seeking to address. Then, include each idea. For the idea, you'll likely need a short title and a longer description to explain it. For instance, you might title an idea "Billing Accuracy" and describe it as "offer a guarantee to customers that our bills will be accurate, or they will receive a refund plus 50% of the error." This will allow you to talk about the idea before building it out.

Broadly, your ideas will fall into the categories of value and maintenance. Generally, but not always, ideas to fill gaps will seek to reduce maintenance and ideas to address opportunities will seek to increase value.

You may find it helpful to organize your ideas into the Purple Goldfish framework at this point. It's certainly not required, but it can help you to compare your ideas to those Purple Goldfish that already exist in the wild.

Value	Maintenance
Throw-Ins	Added Service
Sampling	Convenience
Guarantees	Waiting
Pay It Forward	Handling Mistakes
First and Last Impressions	Follow-up

At this stage, you now have an organized list of gaps and opportunities, along with a list of ideas—the Purple Goldfish Fry—that you can now evaluate. Of course, generating ideas is the easy part. Implementation is much harder.

DESIGN PHASE PROGRESS

✓	**Step One:** Set Your Focus
✓	**Step Two:** Ask Big Questions
✓	**Step Three:** Organize Your Ideas

CHAPTER 22

EVALUATE

Chess masters don't evaluate all the possible moves.
They know how to discard 98 percent of the ones they
could make and then focus on the best choice
of the remaining lot.

- John Dickerson

Y ou may remember that **Evaluate** is the newest part of the I.D.E.A. process. The previous model—the 3Ds of Discover, Design, and Deploy—didn't have enough emphasis on testing ideas before rolling them out. It's not that we didn't advocate for testing before, rather it's that we believe it is now more important than ever.

During the evaluation process, we recommend both internal and external validation. Of course, most of the Purple Goldfish Fry—the ideas—came from people inside your company. Along with the valuable insight each employee brought to the idea came the not-so-valuable biases they inherently have.

In the previous chapter we discussed the concepts of divergent and convergent thinking. At this point in the process, we want to reawaken your convergent thinking ability as our objective is no longer to generate ideas but to determine analytically the viability of each.

With the list of PGFs you generated in the Design phase, you'll now dive into Internal Evaluation.

INTERNAL EVALUATION

Your Internal Evaluation phase starts with the list of PGF you're considering. You'll likely have somewhere between six and ten ideas. You'll want to determine if each of them is likely to work. While we're not yet involving customers, which we'll get to in the next two sections, you'll use this time to evaluate each PGF viability from the company perspective.

Is the idea feasible?

Like many of the concepts we discuss, feasibility studies can be quite complex. We recommend that you use your own judgment as to how thorough you would like for your feasibility study to be. If you're a small business, we recognize that this process might be simple. For a large enterprise, we realize this stage is often where good ideas get stuck. Here are the questions you'll need to answer:

- What resources will be needed to implement this idea? What are the costs associated with those resources?

- Do the costs outweigh the benefits?

- If you're successful, how many of your current customers are likely to take advantage of this Purple Goldfish? Do you expect increased loyalty from these customers?

- If you're successful, how many new customers do you expect this Purple Goldfish may attract?

- Can you expect benefits beyond additional sales and loyalty? Are there any intangible benefits?

It's tempting to think of Internal Evaluation as an elimination round, but we like to think of it as a checkpoint instead. Rather than looking for reasons to eliminate a PGF from consideration, you're looking for reasons to advance it forward. On the other hand, if you find information that leads you to believe the idea is not viable, you have three options. You can either eliminate the PGF, adjust it to be viable, or wait until after external validation to make a final decision.

In either case, you have now evaluated the feasibility of your PGF. We hope your excitement is growing, because the next step is to start getting input from the most important evaluators—your customers.

EVALUATE PHASE PROGRESS

✓	Step One: Internal Evaluation
	Step Two: External Validation
	Step Three: Pilot

EXTERNAL VALIDATION

At this stage, we advocate for two types of input from your customers. The first we call Validation. The idea behind Validation is to use an inexpensive approach for feasibility and avoid the cost of a pilot in the event the idea does not resonate with your customers.

External Validation resembles traditional market research. You'll share your ideas with your target audience and receive their feedback. There's no one correct way to accomplish this, but there are plenty of incorrect ways. Here are some of the ways we recommend seeking input from your customer:

- Focus groups

- Customer advisory board meetings

- Surveys

- One-on-one customer interviews

No matter which research method you choose, you will want to make sure you do a few things. First, you will want to make sure you describe your idea fully to the customer. The title and short description you developed in the Design phase will be helpful, but you may want to include more detail at this stage.

Second, you should get the customers' initial reaction to the idea and then ask if they have any questions about it. First impressions only happen once, so you'll want to capture them immediately.

Third, you'll want to engage further with the customers, asking them what they like and dislike about the idea and if implementation of the idea would cause them to do more business with you. Of course, a positive response is not a guarantee as researchers will tell you. Humans are bad at predicting their future behavior.

Like many of our recommendations, whole books (and dissertations, for that matter) have been written on market research. You may want to pursue DIY research, or you may want to engage a professional researcher or firm. Engaging a researcher or firm will be more expensive, but it may make sense if you have the budget and the stakes are high. If you choose the DIY route, we encourage you to seek out additional resources on market research to guide you.

Once your research is complete, you will need to make decisions about each one of your PGF. You have a few options:

1. Move the PGF into a pilot study

2. Revise the PGF and complete more research

3. Hold the PGF for a future pilot study

4. Eliminate the PGF

You probably will have a mix of all of the above for your project and that's perfectly okay! It's why we do research before rolling out a pilot project. This research most likely generated some additional insights about your customers that you will want to consider during your pilot, or it may cause you to revisit your journey maps with fresh data.

Jack Welch famously said, "An organization's ability to learn, and translate that learning into action rapidly, is the ultimate competitive advantage." Now that you're armed with customer input, you're ready to start putting your ideas into action.

EVALUATE PHASE PROGRESS

✓	Step One: Internal Evaluation
✓	Step Two: External Validation
	Step Three: Pilot

PILOT

We're excited you've made it to the customer-facing Pilot! There's only so much you can learn from the process we've outlined here. Now you get the privilege of learning directly from your customers in a real-world scenario. We are legitimately excited for you!

Pilot programs differ depending upon the size of the organization and customer base. Your Pilot may be as simple as trying out one PGF for a day or as complex as rolling out the PGF in a limited number of your locations for a longer period of time. You're the best judge of what will work most effectively for your customers and organization.

Here are some tips we recommend you keep in mind as you put together your pilot:

- Make sure your pilot is sufficiently sized, by reach or timeframe, to generate a representative sample of your target customers. Keep in mind that your PGF may be targeting a subset of your customers, so you'll want to consider the locations and or timeframes when those customers are most likely to engage.

- Build measurement into the process. As you are planning the pilot, you will want to determine how you'll measure the effects of the PGF. An uptick in sales would be marvelous, but sales may be a lagging indicator. Consider other ways to measure those customers or locations that are part of the Pilot relative to the rest of your customers. Ideally, you would be able to segment the Pilot customers from other customers and compare multiple metrics like survey results, sales, order value/volume, or NPS.

- Make the experience as real as possible. We suggest not telling the customer you are *trying out* something new. Simply say it's something new. In physics, there's a concept called Observer Effect. That is the theory that the mere observation of a phenomenon inevitably changes that phenomenon. We're not physicists, but we do suspect that the knowledge that something is a pilot will change a customer's perception of it.

- Engage in proper training for your team. Remember when outward-facing, it's not a "pilot," it's the new thing. You'll want your team to treat the PGF pilot as normally as possible to avoid skewed results or apathy toward the project.

- Listen to your team. To achieve buy-in and an effective launch, you'll also want to seek the feedback of your team members tasked with delivering your new PGF experience. This input will allow you to head off any opposition or issues that might interrupt an effective roll-out.

Once you deploy the PGF pilot and measure its results, you arrive at your final point of analysis—the go or no-go decision. Next, you'll prepare to roll out any PGF that produces desirable results more widely in your organization. It's PGF graduation day as they're now Purple Goldfish qualified for deployment.

Let's turn our attention to helping you roll them out successfully!

EVALUATE PHASE PROGRESS

✓	Step One: Internal Evaluation
✓	Step Two: External Validation
✓	Step Three: Pilot

CHAPTER 23

ADVANCE

"The difficulties you will meet will resolve themselves as you advance."

- Jim Rohn

Welcome to the last step of the I.D.E.A. process—the **Advance** stage. You may remember that we used to call this the "Deploy" step. Admittedly, we changed the name to better fit the acronym. But in the course of outlining the process, we came to enjoy the concept of advance more, primarily because advancing is something one can do on a continuous basis and deployment is more of a one-time event. Advancing your newly commissioned Purple Goldfish isn't a one-time event. It's a continuous process—one where you seek to advance the Purple Goldfish and the overall experience you create for your customers to a new level.

During the advance stage, you have three primary responsibilities:

    1) Achieve buy-in internally

    2) Roll out the experience to customers

    3) Set up a feedback loop with continuous measurement

BUY-IN

Every organization operates differently, and your buy-in process will differ accordingly. As a small company, you may only need to achieve buy-in from a small group. For larger companies, you may have a formal review process and a need to achieve approval from a number of stakeholders. As with considering or implementing any of our advice, you know your organization best, so we're not in a position to be prescriptive about what buy-in you will need to achieve.

We do believe, however, that there are common components of achieving buy-in, so we recommend that you take all of them into account:

- **Communicate the plan with the right stakeholders.** You'll want to make sure that everyone who has influence over the project is on-board. Don't forget the influence that teams like operations and finance can wield—involve them as early as possible and ensure you address their concerns.

- **Don't forget your front-line employees.** These are the people tasked with implementing the Purple Goldfish, so their understanding of both why and how to deploy the Purple Goldfish is essential.

- **Present the story of the idea.** It might be tempting to say, "We decided to do this, and these are the results." While that is true, a significant amount or work went into formulating the PGF throughout the Inquire, Design, and Evaluate phases. Make sure everyone knows how the Purple Goldfish came to be.

- **Use anecdotes to win hearts.** During your pilot project, you no doubt heard anecdotal feedback of how the Purple Goldfish helped a customer. By sharing some of that feedback, you will connect with and engender empathy (and usually support) from your stakeholders.

- **Use data to win minds.** Thinking back to the discussion about convergent thinking, you know you'll need numbers to prove that the Purple Goldfish was successful. You gathered significant data from the pilot, so use it to share (and prove) what you learned.

- **Present adjustments based on pilot feedback.** A story where everything is perfect not only isn't believable, it's boring. You'll want to present some of the learnings from your pilot as well as the adjustments they necessitated to solidify buy-in.

We can't guarantee an easy buy-in process if you follow these tips, but we can guarantee that you'll set yourself up for success. Once you achieve buy-in, the most fun part comes next—rolling your Purple Goldfish out to customers!

ADVANCE PHASE PROGRESS

✓	Step One: Buy-In
	Step Two: Rollout
	Step Three: Measurement

ROLLOUT

Let's do this! Rollout is one of the most exciting and critical parts of the journey. You'll soon see the fruits of your labor, but to do so you'll need a successful rollout. Just as in each of the previous phases, how you roll out your Purple Goldfish will be based on your organization, the resources involved, and any number of other factors. Much as before, this leaves us to offer our generalized guidance. We encourage you to adapt as necessary to suit your needs.

Here are some of the factors you should consider during rollout:

- **Communication** – How will you communicate the Purple Goldfish offering to both front-line employees and customers?

- **Policies** – How clear are your policies regarding what is allowed and disallowed? Have you considered edge cases or exceptions?

- **Logistics** – What new materials need to be acquired and distributed to the front-line?

- **Metrics** – How will you collect relevant metrics? You measured during your pilot, so you already have a start. How will standard measurement differ from your pilot?

- **Promotion** – As you know from reading this book, we don't advocate for Purple Goldfish as a PR strategy, but you may need to promote the offering to gain initial usage from customers.

Rollout may seem simple, however, it is anything but. How well you roll out your Purple Goldfish may determine its fate. This time might be marked by late nights and early mornings, but all of the work you've done up to this point should provide the necessary motivation to make it happen. We believe in you (and your Purple Goldfish)!

ADVANCE PHASE PROGRESS

✓	Step One: Buy-In
✓	Step Two: Rollout
	Step Three: Measurement

MEASUREMENT

As you know from the pilot, measurement is how you prove your Purple Goldfish is working and delivering the desired results for the business. Measurement is also how you gain valuable insights that will help you return to the Inquire phase and address new (or different) gaps and opportunities. Here are some of our tips for effective measurement, realizing, as you know by now, that every organization is different.

- **Collect performance data.** You identified the metrics as a part of the rollout, so now you'll want to collect and analyze the data.

- **Use segmentation to understand relative performance.** Over time the enthusiastic buy-in you achieved may wane, so you'll want to show how the Purple Goldfish consistently delivers results. Ideally, you will be able to compare key metrics between those customers who experience the Purple Goldfish and those who did not.

- **Mind the bottom line.** You'll want to connect the performance of the Purple Goldfish to metrics as close to the bottom line as possible. By showing increased loyalty and profitability because of the Purple Goldfish, you're likely to retain the necessary support to keep the goldfish swimming. (No apologies for the pun.)

- **Refine as needed.** There's no reason you can't tweak as you go along. Despite the best planning and analysis, your Purple Goldfish may miss the mark slightly. Don't hesitate to make adjustments as needed but resist the urge to make them too early. There's no right answer here, so follow your gut. It's usually right.

- **Build the feedback loop.** Continue collecting the necessary data to loop back to the Inquire phase. As you improve, the desire to improve will grow in your organization. Use this desire, your new data, and, hopefully, your new profits to fuel the feedback loop. This will create a flywheel effect that allows your organization to reach new heights on a continuous basis.

Woohoo! You've made it through the I.D.E.A. Process! Our excitement level is high, because we know that with every Purple Goldfish out in the wild, there's a customer somewhere whose experience is just a little better than it was before. It's why we do what we do, and we hope you share the same excitement.

ADVANCE PHASE PROGRESS

✓	Step One: Buy-In
✓	Step Two: Rollout
✓	Step Three: Measurement

WHAT HAPPENS NEXT?

Your goal is to consistently move to the next plateau on each iteration through the I.D.E.A. Process. As we've said, a Purple Goldfish isn't a campaign—it's a commitment. What was once a differentiator can quickly become an expectation, so consistent improvement is essential in today's hyper-competitive marketplace. New successes come with increased expectations, which bring up new issues. It's not just about completing the I.D.E.A. Process again, it's about consistently serving the customer.

PART IV

FINAL THOUGHTS

CHAPTER 24

TOP 12 KEY
TAKEAWAYS

"Advice is like a tablet of aspirin.
It only works if you actually take it."

- David Murphy

LET US COUNT THE TOP 12 MOST IMPORTANT TAKEAWAYS FROM PURPLE GOLDFISH 2.0:

#1. THE BIGGEST MYTH IN MARKETING

There is no such thing as meeting expectations. You either exceed them or you fall short.

#2. CHOOSE WISELY

You can't be all things to all people. You only have two choices as a marketer: create to spec and face being a commodity or set out to exceed expectations and become remarkable.

#3. SHAREHOLDERS VS. CUSTOMERS?

Business is about creating and keeping customers, not just serving shareholder interests. Customer experience should be priority #1 in your marketing. Stop focusing on the "two in the bush" (prospects) and take care of the one in your hand (customers).

#4. VALUE IS THE NEW BLACK

Don't compete on price. Cater to the 70% who buy based on value. Price is only relative to the value received.

#5. PHELPS COROLLARY TO THE PARETO PRINCIPLE

Traditional marketing is flawed. Eighty percent of your efforts will net 20 percent of your results. Focus on existing customers instead of the funnel by finding little extras that are tangible, valuable, and talkable to delight them.

#6. GROWTH IS DETERMINED BY FIVE FACTORS

The growth of your product or service is similar to that of a gold-fish. Growth is determined by 5 factors: size of the bowl (Market), number of other goldfish in the bowl (Competition), quality of the water in the bowl (Business Environment / Economy), first 120 Days of life (Start-up), and Genetic make-up (Differentiation). Assuming you've already been in business for four months, the only thing you can control is how you differentiate yourself.

#7. PURPLE GOLDFISH STRATEGY

Purple Goldfish Strategy is "differentiation via added value"—finding signature extras that help you stand out, improve customer experience, reduce attrition, and drive positive word of mouth.

#8. ACTS OF KINDNESS

Think of lagniappe as an added branded act of kindness. A beacon or sign that shows you care. Marketing via G.L.U.E (giving little unexpected extras). A little something thrown in for good measure.

#9. LAGNIAPPE ECONOMY

There is a middle ground between a Market Economy (quid pro quo) and a Gift Economy (free). A lagniappe economy is where there is an exchange of goods and services for an exact value (market economy) plus a little unexpected extra that is given for good measure (gift economy).

#10. V4 PRINCIPLE

v4 is when a consumer becomes a PROsumer. They stand up for a product or service and vouch for it, giving personal assurances to its value. As a marketer you need to figure out a way to make your product or service "remark-able." Are you giving your customers something to talk, tweet, blog, and post to Facebook about?

#11. FIVE INGREDIENTS

Here's a reminder of the five ingredients or R.U.L.E.S. of a Purple Goldfish:

- **R**elevant - The extra should be of value to the recipient.

- **U**nexpected - It should "surprise and delight."

- **L**imited - The extra should be something rare, hard to find, or signature to your business.

- **E**xpressive - It should be a sign that you care.

- **S**ticky - It should be memorable and talkable.

#12. VALUE / MAINTENANCE MATRIX

The VM matrix calculates how a brand measures up on two important criteria: value and maintenance. The goal is to be seen as "high value" and "low maintenance" by your customers. As a reminder, here are the 10 types of Purple Goldfish based on value and maintenance:

Add Value	Reduce Maintenance
Throw-Ins	Added Service
Sampling	Convenience
Guarantees	Waiting
Pay It Forward	Handling Mistakes
First and Last Impressions	Follow-up

FINAL THOUGHTS

We hope you enjoyed this book. In closing, allow us to make five final points about Purple Goldfish.

YOU CAN'T MAKE CHICKEN SALAD...

You can't make chicken salad out of chicken crap. Creating a Purple Goldfish is not a substitute for having a strong product or service. Get the basics right before considering the little unexpected extras.

AUTHENTIC VS. FORCED

A Purple Goldfish is a beacon. A small gift or offering that demonstrates you care. It needs to be done in an authentic way. If it comes across as forced or contrived, you'll eliminate all of the goodwill and negatively impact your product or service.

A DAILY REGIMEN OF EXERCISE VS. LIPOSUCTION

Purple Goldfish is not a quick fix or for those seeking immediate results. Translation: it's not liposuction. It's equivalent to working out every day. The results gradually build and improve over time.

IT'S A COMMITMENT, NOT A CAMPAIGN

A Purple Goldfish is different than a promotion or limited time offer. It's a feature that becomes embedded into the fabric of your product or service. Add one or a school of goldfish at your convenience; remove them at your peril.

EVERY GREAT JOURNEY BEGINS WITH A SINGLE STEP

Start small when adding a signature extra and add gradually. The best brands are those who boast a whole school of Purple Goldfish.

ADDITIONAL READING
WE RECOMMEND

99.3 Random Acts of Marketing by Drew McLellan

Delivering Happiness by Tony Hsieh

Domino by Linda Ireland

Five Star Customer Service by Ted Coiné

FREE by Chris Anderson

Giftology by John Ruland

Hug Your Customers by Jack Mitchell

Killing Giants by Stephen Denny

My Story by Stew Leonard

Purple Cow by Seth Godin

Talk Triggers by Jay Baer and Daniel Lemin

The End of Business as Usual by Brian Solis

The Experience Effect by Jim Joseph

The Next Evolution of Marketing by Bob Gilbreath

The Power of Moments by Chip and Dan Heath

The Thank You Economy by Gary Vaynerchuk

Tipping Point by Malcolm Gladwell

Winning the Customer by Lou Imbriano

ABOUT THE AUTHORS

STAN PHELPS

Stan Phelps is a best-selling author, keynote speaker, and workshop facilitator. He believes that today's organizations must focus on meaningful differentiation to win the hearts of both employees and customers.

He is the founder of PurpleGoldfish.com. Purple Goldfish is a think tank of customer experience and employee engagement experts that offers keynotes and workshops that drive loyalty and sales. The group helps organizations connect with the hearts and minds of customers and employees.

Prior to PurpleGoldfish.com, Stan had a 20-year career in marketing that included leadership positions at IMG, adidas, PGA Exhibitions, and Synergy. At Synergy, he worked on award-winning experiential programs for top brands such as KFC, Wachovia, NASCAR, Starbucks, and M&M's.

Stan is a TEDx speaker, a Forbes contributor, and an IBM Futurist. His writing is syndicated on top sites such as Customer Think and Business2Community. He has spoken at more than 400 events across Australia, Bahrain, Canada, Ecuador, France, Germany, Holland, Israel, Japan, Malaysia, Peru, Russia, Singapore, Spain, Sweden, UK, and the US.

He is the author of 9 other business books and one fun one:

- *Green Goldfish 2.0 - 15 Keys to Driving Employee Engagement*

- *Golden Goldfish - The Vital Few*

- *Blue Goldfish - Using Technology, Data, and Analytics to Drive Both Profits and Prophets*

- *Purple Goldfish Service Edition - 12 Ways Hotels, Restaurants, and Airlines Win the Right Customers*

- *Red Goldfish - Motivating Sales and Loyalty Through Shared Passion and Purpose*

- *Pink Goldfish - Defy Normal, Exploit Imperfection, and Captivate Your Customers*

- *Purple Goldfish Franchise Edition - The Ultimate S.Y.S.T.E.M. for Franchisors and Franchisees*

- *Yellow Goldfish - Nine Ways to Drive Happiness in Business for Growth, Productivity, and Prosperity*

- *Gray Goldfish - Navigating the Gray Areas to Successfully Lead Every Generation*

- *Bar Tricks, Bad Jokes, & Even Worse Stories*

Stan received a BS in Marketing and Human Resources from Marist College, a JD/MBA from Villanova University, and a certificate for Achieving Breakthrough Service from Harvard Business School. He is a Certified Net Promoter Associate and has taught as an adjunct professor at NYU, Rutgers University, and Manhattanville College. Stan is also a fellow at Maddock Douglas, an innovation consulting firm in Chicago. Stan lives in Cary, North Carolina, with his wife, Jennifer, and their two boys, Thomas and James.

To book Stan for an upcoming keynote, webinar, or workshop go to stanphelpsspeaks.com. You can reach Stan at stan@purplegoldfish. com or call +1.919.360.4702 or follow him on Twitter: @StanPhelpsPG.

EVAN CARROLL

Evan helps companies innovate with the right blend of tech-driven and human-to-human interactions. The result is a win-win-win— that's an experience that's better for customers, employees, and the bottom line. He has spoken at a wide range of events ranging from the trend-setting South by Southwest conference to a national forum at the Library of Congress.

As the author of multiple books, Evan has appeared in major news outlets including *The New York Times,* CBS Sunday Morning, NPR's *Fresh Air, The Atlantic,* and *Popular Science.*

Evan's other books provide a human-centric view of emerging issues in technology and business. *Blue Goldfish* is based on over 300 examples of how to develop customer relationships, improve responsiveness, and increase overall readiness to meet customer needs. *Your Digital Afterlife* is the first book ever to address what happens to our digital lives when we pass away.

With a career spanning roles in user experience design, marketing, and product management, Evan has contributed to the success of leading agencies and technology companies, including IBM, Ketchum, and ChannelAdvisor.

He practices what he preaches through his firm Attended, which specializes in experience design and production. Recognizing his dedication to the field, the AMA named Evan its National Volunteer of the Year in 2017.

Evan holds MS and BS degrees in Information Science from UNC-Chapel Hill, where he now serves as an adjunct professor.

To book Evan for an upcoming keynote or workshop please visit www.evancarroll.net. You can reach Evan at evan@evancarroll.net or call +1.919.442.8799 or follow him on Twitter: @evancarroll.

OTHER COLORS IN THE GOLDFISH SERIES

GREEN GOLDFISH 2.0 – 15 KEYS TO DRIVING EMPLOYEE ENGAGEMENT

Green Goldfish is based on the simple premise that "happy engaged employees create happy enthused customers." The book focuses on 15 different ways to drive employee engagement and reinforce a strong corporate culture.

GOLDEN GOLDFISH – THE VITAL FEW

Golden Goldfish examines the importance of your top 20 percent of customers and employees. The book showcases nine ways to drive loyalty and retention with these two critical groups.

BLUE GOLDFISH - USING TECHNOLOGY, DATA, AND ANALYTICS TO DRIVE BOTH PROFITS AND PROPHETS

Blue Goldfish examines how to leverage technology, data, and analytics to do a "little something extra" to improve the experience for the customer. The book is based on a collection of over 300 case studies. It examines the three R's: Relationship, Responsiveness, and Readiness. *Blue Goldfish* uncovers eight different ways to turn insights into action.

RED GOLDFISH - MOTIVATING SALES AND LOYALTY THROUGH SHARED PASSION AND PURPOSE

Purpose is changing the way we work and how customers choose business partners. It is driving loyalty, and it's on its way to becoming the ultimate differentiator in business. *Red Goldfish* shares cutting edge examples and reveals the eight ways businesses can embrace purpose that drives employee engagement, fuels the bottom line, and makes an impact on the lives of those it serves.

PURPLE GOLDFISH SERVICE EDITION - 12 WAYS HOTELS, RESTAURANTS, AND AIRLINES WIN THE RIGHT CUSTOMERS

Purple Goldfish Service Edition is about differentiation via added value, and marketing to your existing customers via G.L.U.E. (**g**iving **l**ittle **u**nexpected **e**xtras). Packed with over 100 examples, the book focuses on the 12 ways to do the "little extras" to improve the customer experience for restaurants, hotels, and airlines. The end result is increased sales, happier customers, and positive word of mouth.

PINK GOLDFISH - DEFY NORMAL, EXPLOIT IMPERFECTION, AND CAPTIVATE YOUR CUSTOMERS

Companies need to stand out in a crowded marketplace, but true differentiation is increasingly rare. Based on over 200 case studies, *Pink Goldfish* provides an unconventional seven-part framework for achieving competitive separation by embracing flaws instead of fixing them.

PURPLE GOLDFISH FRANCHISE EDITION - THE ULTIMATE S.Y.S.T.E.M. FOR FRANCHISORS AND FRANCHISEES

Packed with over 100 best-practice examples, *Purple Goldfish Franchise Edition* focuses on the six keys to creating a successful franchise S.Y.S.T.E.M. and a dozen ways to create a signature customer experience.

YELLOW GOLDFISH - NINE WAYS TO DRIVE HAPPINESS IN BUSINESS FOR GROWTH, PRODUCTIVITY, AND PROSPERITY

There should only be one success metric in business and that's happiness. A Yellow Goldfish is any time a business does a little extra to contribute to the happiness of its customers, employees, or society. Based on nearly 300 case studies, *Yellow Goldfish* provides a nine-part framework for happiness-driven growth, productivity, and prosperity in business.

GRAY GOLDFISH - NAVIGATING THE GRAY AREAS TO SUCCESSFULLY LEAD EVERY GENERATION

How do you successfully lead the five generations in today's workforce? You need tools to navigate. Filled with over 100 case studies and the Generational Matrix, *Gray Goldfish* provides the definitive map for leaders to follow as they recruit, train, manage, and inspire across the generations.

Made in the USA
Monee, IL
04 July 2023

38522080R00148